The strength of this book is rooted in Cunni[n...]
church's engagement with pressing contempo[rary...]
God as Trinity and the display of God's natur[e...]
that the gospel of Jesus Christ is the solution [to all the issues that face the]
church today.
—**Samuel Boateng**, West Africa Catalyst, City to City Africa

Ralph Cunnington has offered us a great gift for growing in grace and truth. Rooted in Robert Letham's "distinct but inseparable" formula for examining biblical truth, and drawing deeply on both patristic and Reformed traditions, Cunnington proves to be a clear and trustworthy teacher of central doctrines in our faith and a seasoned pastoral guide through some of the most vital conversations Christians engage in today. *Perfect Unity* isn't simply an able explanation of the Bible's teaching concerning God, the world, and the gospel but a wise handbook on how these truths are applied to answer some of the most pressing questions of our time, including identity, gender, holiness, and the fabric of community in the church. *Perfect Unity* is a must-read. I commend it to all with prayers for its every fruitfulness on both sides of the Atlantic and beyond.
—**David Cassidy**, Senior Pastor, Spanish River Church, Boca Raton, Florida

In many of our pressing concerns, there is a delicate dance between unity and diversity. How can we honor a tapestry of difference while cherishing the threads that hold it together? How can we differentiate without risking fragmentation? Ralph Cunnington adeptly contends that the biblical blueprint offers a compelling solution: the profound truth that entities can be distinct yet inseparable. *Perfect Unity* not only equips us to navigate today's most contentious issues but also guides us on a transformative journey as Christians, leading us to a deeper, revitalized worship of the God who embodies unity in diversity.
—**Pete Dray**, Interim Executive Director, UCCF: The Christian Unions

You notice a loose thread and instinctively begin to pull it. Then you realize that disaster is imminent; you are in danger of unravelling the whole garment. But if you keep pulling, you will discover how the cloth has been woven together.

Is it worth continuing to pull? In *Perfect Unity*, Ralph Cunnington skillfully shows us that when it comes to the Christian faith, there is a loose thread that is worth pulling. Why? Because this thread will help us appreciate how beautifully God has woven the gospel—what John Calvin called "the garment" in which Christ has clothed himself. So what is this "loose thread"? The answer may surprise you. It is "distinct but inseparable." Intrigued? Then read on!
—**Sinclair B. Ferguson**, Chancellor's Professor of Systematic Theology, Reformed Theological Seminary

In a world frayed by polarization and divisiveness, *Perfect Unity* invites the reader to begin and end by looking up at the Godhead, our reference point for unity in diversity. It is a concise and accessible primer ideal for small groups to unpack core sound doctrines that will lead to sound, or healthy, lives and churches.
—**Karen Hodge**, Women's Ministry Coordinator, Presbyterian Church in America

Humanity is destined to live in love across lines of deep difference. This destiny is rooted in the beauty of our triune God, who is eternally existent as beautiful community, the perfection of unity in diversity and diversity in unity. Despite this truth, Christians are still struggling to persevere in pursuing beautiful community to the glory of God. We continue to need faithful servants of the Lord to lay a clear path for us to follow. In *Perfect Unity*, Pastor Ralph Cunnington systematically and practically grounds us in the knowledge of God, the implications for our life together as his people, and the way we bear witness for beauty in a confused and broken world. May God be pleased to bear much fruit for his glory for those who heed the wisdom in this book!
—**Irwyn L. Ince Jr.**, Author, *The Beautiful Community*

Brilliant and concise, rooted in pastoral experience, with an abundance of striking examples, this is a great book for new Christians and older ones alike. Cunnington's argument provides a key to unlocking many of the central doctrines of the faith.
—**Robert Letham**, Professor of Systematic and Historical Theology, Union School of Theology

Ralph Cunnington writes with the theological precision of a professor and the sensitivity of a seasoned pastor. As I read *Perfect Unity*, I found myself rejoicing in the depth and beauty of the triune God and his creation. The book explains deep theological truth with clarity, accessibility, and power. Cunnington convincingly argues that unity in the midst of diversity is the footprint God left all over his creation and that understanding the distinct but inseparable unity of the triune God lifts us above the confusion of our present day to worship the everlasting God in all his glory. This excellent book will be a resource I use again and again in small groups and discipleship.
—**Jenny Manley**, Author, *The Good Portion: Christ*

The great contemporary challenge that faces humanity is how to achieve real unity without obliterating our diversity. Ralph Cunnington shows that the answer to this conundrum is not to be found in secular philosophies and ideologies but in the core truths of the Christian faith, which reveal the principle of "distinct but inseparable." Expounding Scripture and drawing on many of the great theologians of church history, he shows that this principle is ultimately rooted in the eternal Trinitarian nature of God, embodied in the person of Christ and worked out in our salvation and the Christian life. Accessibly but not simplistically, he examines creation, justification, sanctification, and the church and shows how they all reflect the "distinct but inseparable" paradigm. He helpfully shows how this provides a better framework for overcoming division in hotly contested areas such as race and gender. Readers will gain a fresh perspective that will enable them to relate their faith to our cultural context with confidence and a renewed longing for the coming of God's kingdom of perfect peace and unity. It will guard us against the perennial danger of separating what God has joined together.
—**John Stevens**, National Director, Fellowship of Independent Evangelical Churches

This is a great introduction to Christian doctrine—not too light, not too heavy, but just right. The running theme of "distinct but inseparable" is both profound and memorable, and the discussion questions make it suitable for both individuals and groups. Recommended.
—**Dan Strange**, Director, Crosslands Forum

PERFECT UNITY

PERFECT UNITY

A Guide for
Christian Doctrine and Life

RALPH CUNNINGTON

P&R
PUBLISHING
P.O. BOX 817 • PHILLIPSBURG • NEW JERSEY 08865-0817

© 2024 by Ralph Cunnington

All rights reserved. No part of this book may be reproduced, stored in a retrieval system, or transmitted in any form or by any means—electronic, mechanical, photocopy, recording, or otherwise—except for brief quotations for the purpose of review or comment, without the prior permission of the publisher, P&R Publishing Company, P.O. Box 817, Phillipsburg, New Jersey 08865-0817.

Unless otherwise indicated, Scripture quotations are from the Holy Bible, New International Version®, NIV®. Copyright © 1973, 1978, 1984, 2011 by Biblica, Inc.™ Used by permission of Zondervan. All rights reserved worldwide. www.zondervan.com. The "NIV" and "New International Version" are trademarks registered in the United States Patent and Trademark Office by Biblica, Inc.™

Scripture quotations marked (ESV) are from the ESV® Bible (The Holy Bible, English Standard Version®), copyright © 2001 by Crossway, a publishing ministry of Good News Publishers. Used by permission. All rights reserved.

Italics within Scripture quotations indicate emphasis added.

Cover design by Jelena Mirkovic

Printed in the United States of America

Library of Congress Cataloging-in-Publication Data

Names: Cunnington, Ralph, author.
Title: Perfect unity : a guide for Christian doctrine and life / Ralph Cunnington.
Description: Phillipsburg, New Jersey : P&R Publishing, [2024] | Summary: "Perfect unity. Oneness that doesn't erase difference. Examining God, the Gospel, the Christian life, and more, Cunnington shows how the theme of distinction without separation unlocks doctrine and enables true community"-- Provided by publisher.
Identifiers: LCCN 2023048149 | ISBN 9781629958552 (paperback) | ISBN 9781629958590 (epub)
Subjects: LCSH: Theology, Doctrinal--Popular works.
Classification: LCC BT77 .C8424 2024 | DDC 230--dc23/eng/20231227
LC record available at https://lccn.loc.gov/2023048149

CONTENTS

Foreword by Scotty Smith	vii
Acknowledgments	ix
Introduction	xi

Part 1: Who Is God?

1. One God in Three Persons	3
2. The Relational Trinity	11
3. The Distinct but Inseparable Trinity	19

Part 2: What Is the Gospel?

4. Creation and Fall	29
5. Redemption	39
6. Restoration	51

Part 3: What Is Happening in the World?

7. God's Sovereignty and Human Responsibility	61
8. The Dynamic of Sovereignty and Responsibility	71
9. Living Responsibly under God's Sovereignty	81

Part 4: What Is a Christian?

10. Christian Identity	93
11. Gospel Gifts	99
12. Past, Present, and Future	113

Part 5: How Does a Christian Grow?
13. The Ministry of the Sacraments   127
14. The Ministry of the Word   137

Part 6: What Is the Church?
15. One Church with Many Gifts   151
16. One Church with Two Genders   159
17. One Church of All Nations   175

   Conclusion   193
   Glossary   197

FOREWORD

I love Ralph's new book, period. Let's start right there. It is now my favorite introduction to the God of the Bible, overview of the unfolding story the Bible tells, and exploration of the riches and implications of the gospel of Jesus Christ. It is accessible, timely, and intelligent. It is rooted in historical orthodoxy and is as current as the challenges of our day. And somehow, Ralph was able to pull all that off in just over two hundred pages.

Even if I didn't share a treasured friendship with Ralph and had simply discovered his new book online or in a friend's home, the title *Perfect Unity* would have instantly piqued my interest. In an age of divisiveness, enmity, and strife, even semi-healthy expressions of unity are desperately needed. And though the concept of "perfect unity" seems implausible, as a Christian I am wired for hope. So the title rocks.

But the subtitle is just as compelling to me personally—maybe even more so. As someone who has been directionally impaired all my life, the word *guide* brings me comfort—especially when it's connected to matters of faith and life. I discovered a long time ago that there's nothing *more than* the gospel, just *more of* the gospel. So I'm always ready to be guided into a greater understanding and experience of "the faith delivered once for all to the saints" (Jude 1:3).

But as awesome as the title of Ralph's book may be, the title is #5 on a top five list of reasons I am excited and grateful for this new book.

Before I ever turned one page of Ralph's manuscript, I experienced the reality that generated the sentences, paragraphs, and chapters of this wonderful book. Indeed, I saw, smelled, and tasted this book before I read it. I witnessed organic reality before I interacted with my friend's thoughts on paper. It's impossible for me to overstate how important of a gift this is to me. I have had the privilege of both visiting and ministering in City Church Manchester, where Ralph serves as lead pastor.

Nothing narrated in these pages is abstract theory but is rather gospel reality in the making. It's a lot easier to write an aspirational book about unity than chronicle God's work in creating palpable unity in your own highly diverse church family. Ralph has a well-trained mind, but he also has a grace-trained palate—savoring the present reality of God's kingdom, while he hungers for the fullness of the kingdom. It shows up in his pastoring and his writing.

Indeed, I thank God for City Church—a community that demonstrates that unity isn't uniformity, a big group hug, and the absence of conflict. Unity is the blending, not homogenizing, of the grand diversity we enjoy as image bearers of God. Ralph's book shows us that this unity is grounded in the greatness, oneness, and diversity of God himself—as Father, Son, and Holy Spirit—and is brought to life by the person and work of Jesus and the present ministry of the Holy Spirit.

As I read *Perfect Unity*, it increasingly felt as though I were enjoying a musical score. This book sings as much as it informs. It doesn't just present the truth but also opens the curtains on the goodness and beauty of our God and his glorious gospel. Thank you, Ralph. Thank you, my dear friend, brother, and colleague in gospel wonder. Your church family, heart, book, and title all rock.

Scotty Smith
Franklin, Tennessee

ACKNOWLEDGMENTS

It has been said that "it takes a village to raise a child," and it certainly takes a church to raise a Christian author. I would therefore like to thank various people who have shaped me and, in so doing, shaped this book. First, I thank my academic mentor, Dr. Bob Letham, without whom this book would never have been written. I am so grateful for your input at various stages of the project. My spiritual mentor, Scotty Smith, has been a constant presence. My heart is daily warmed by your gospel nuggets, and you have cheered me on throughout the writing of this book. Thank you.

Thanks also to Tessa Reed, Helen Hughes, Brandon O'Brien, Matt Waldock, and Emma Cunnington, who read earlier drafts of the book and gave invaluable feedback. Thank you for your keen eye and for improving the book in so many ways. Tessa also provided the questions at the end of each chapter, which I trust will help readers to dig deeper and apply what they have read to their own lives.

I am immensely blessed to be a pastor and a member of City Church Manchester. We are only nine years old as a church, but God has done so many wonderful things in and through us. I love our diversity (over forty nations) and our unity (we only split in order to plant churches), and I'm deeply aware that these are gifts from God. Thank you to my fellow elders, Matt, Josh, Eric, Boaz, and Sam, who covered for me while I wrote this book on sabbatical.

Thank you to P&R Publishing, and especially to Amanda Martin, Joy Woo, David Acevedo, John Hughes, and Dave Almack, who shaped and guided this book on its road to completion. All errors remain my own.

Lastly, I would like to thank my family. Sophie, Zach, and Jacob, you bring fun, laughter, and joy into my life. I love the way you are so different and yet such great friends. And Anna, my distinct but inseparable companion: thank you for your love, support, and kindness. It is always more than I deserve. Thank you for reminding me daily of the gospel of grace through your grace-driven love for me.

Soli Deo gloria in this book and in his one church—distinct but inseparable.

INTRODUCTION

John Lennon urged us to "imagine": imagine a world where there are no countries, where we all live in peace, where we all live as *one*. I find that vision pretty appealing. I love the idea of the world, in all its beautiful diversity, being united—each part playing its role, retaining its unique features while contributing to the one, unified whole.

But as I look around, I see a world rife with division. There is conflict between countries and conflict within countries. Despots order their armies to commit atrocious acts in order to realign ancient boundaries. Neighbors and family members turn against one another as they align themselves with different group identities that are defined by what they oppose. It is ugly, and it is sad. We yearn for the sort of "oneness" that Lennon describes, but it seems tantalizingly elusive. Is there any hope?

Lennon's answer, in his song "Imagine," is an atheistic utopia that channels Marx and Engel's *Communist Manifesto*: a place where there is no heaven, hell, or religion. For many people, this may sound persuasive. After all, religion has been at the root of many of the world's worst conflicts. Whether it be the hostility between Shi'a and Sunni Muslims in the Middle East, the tragic complicity of the Protestant church in the African slave trade, or the marginalization of same-sex-attracted people by the church, the role of religion in dividing us is undeniable.

It is misguided, however, to assume that the solution to division on earth is simply to remove religion and replace it with a form of philosophical naturalism. Indeed, the nihilism that Lennon proposes fails both to accurately diagnose the problem and to offer a viable solution.

Introduction

Let's start with the problem, which we can observe on both an individual and a societal level.

As individuals, we encounter a curious paradox: we fear difference, and yet we are strangely drawn to it. I see that in my marriage. Anna and I are a prime example of the saying "opposites attract." Our personalities, interests, love languages, and approaches to conflict are all at opposite ends of the spectrum, and that is one of the things that so attracts us to one another. Yet, at times, it is also a source of fear because differences expose.

Engaging with someone who is different from you shines a light on your personality, assumptions, culture, and desires. Because it can be profoundly unsettling, it often makes us yearn for an echo chamber—for people who are just like us. We also see these impulses in relations between people of different ethnicities. Initially, we may find it intriguing to learn about other people's languages, customs, histories, and cuisines. But before long, we become uncomfortable as our assumptions are challenged and the views we hold strongly are exposed as culturally formed preferences.

We see the same dynamic at work in society. In the 1970s, multiculturalism was a settled government policy in the United Kingdom. It was seen as the best way to accommodate the significant increase in postwar immigration. The government assumed that communities would be able to live side by side without adapting any of their cultures, languages, or customs. More recently, however, this approach has been called into question. The inability of communities to peacefully coexist, along with real concerns about what some groups believe, has resulted in greater opposition to multiculturalism. The former head of the Commission for Racial Equality, Trevor Phillips, stated that "multiculturalism suggests separateness" and that the UK needs a more unifying and homogeneous culture with "common values . . . the common currency of the English language, honouring the culture of these islands, like Shakespeare and Dickens."[1]

This is a controversial topic—and multiculturalism is a notoriously difficult concept to define—but it highlights the uncomfortable truth that diversity is both attractive and repellant, beautiful and unsettling.

---

1. Anushka Asthana and Gaby Hinsliff, "Equality Chief Branded as 'Right Wing,'" *The Guardian*, April 3, 2004, https://www.theguardian.com/uk/2004/apr/04/race.britishidentity.

Why is that so?

John Lennon's musings in "Imagine" fail to make sense of the problem. His naturalistic account of the world, in which we are nothing more than impersonal atoms flying around and bumping into one another, does not explain why we value diversity and find it so attractive. His insistence that the problem lies with established religion overlooks its true source: our own hearts. This, of course, means that the concepts of heaven and hell cannot be so easily discarded.

What is the solution? For a time, society (under the influence of modernism) sought to pursue unity by denying difference. Abraham Kuyper memorably described this as "a reckless levelling and the elimination of all diversity," which "seeks a false, deceptive unity, the uniformity of death."[2] Kuyper traced this tendency from the Roman Empire to the French Revolution: "Blind to the rich profusion of the different shades of life, it crushes everything fresh and natural by its thirst for the conventional."[3] He saw it in his own day through the erosion of ethnic, cultural, and sexual distinctions. His work was remarkably prophetic and anticipated the late twentieth century, in which claims to be "gender blind" and "color blind" were lauded rather than condemned.

Things have changed since then. Today, society (under the influence of postmodernism) has chosen to emphasize difference rather than deny it. One manifestation of this has been the emergence of identity politics, which establishes alternating power structures in which one group oppresses the other and then is oppressed by it in turn. The background to this conceptualization of society has been historic and documented injustice (both individual and structural) that requires redress.

To this extent, the motivation of many who swim in the waters of identity politics is both good and biblical. Scripture is clear that the Lord cares for the marginalized and the oppressed (see Isa. 25:4; 61:1–3; Mal. 3:5) and that Christians should too (see Isa. 1:17; Zech. 7:9–10). The problem is that identity politics not only seeks to right historic wrongs but also creates distance between people groups and pits them against one another: men against women, Whites against Blacks, transgender people against feminists. Consistent with

---

2. Abraham Kuyper, "Uniformity: The Curse of Modern Life," in *Abraham Kuyper: A Centennial Reader*, ed. James D. Bratt (Grand Rapids: Eerdmans, 1998), 23.
3. Kuyper, 25.

its postmodern underpinnings, identity politics is excellent at celebrating and even intensifying diversity, but it has no framework for establishing unity.

In short, the modern approach denies the glory of diversity, while the postmodern approach denies the possibility of unity. We instinctively long for something better: true unity amid true diversity. Yet this always seems out of reach. Is there any hope? In his classic work *Mere Christianity*, C. S. Lewis famously wrote,

> The Christian says, Creatures are not born with desires unless satisfaction for those desires exists. A baby feels hunger: well, there is such a thing as food. A duckling wants to swim: well, there is such a thing as water. Men feel sexual desire: well, there is such a thing as sex. If I find in myself a desire which no experience in this world can satisfy, the most probable explanation is that I was made for another world. If none of my earthly pleasures satisfy it, that does not prove that the universe is a fraud. Probably earthly pleasures were never meant to satisfy it, but only to arouse it, to suggest the real thing.[4]

What if our desire for unity in diversity points beyond our observable experience to a reality that is found within God himself? And what if this reality could become ours by being caught up into the beautiful story that Christians call the gospel?

The seed of this book was planted more than a decade ago. I remember it well. Our second child, Zach, had just been born and was keeping my wife and me up at night. It was my first year at the Wales Evangelical School of Theology (now Union School of Theology), and, determined not to miss any lectures, I made my way to my 9 a.m. systematic theology class. As I took my seat, Dr. Robert Letham announced, "These three words will stand you in good stead as you continue theological study and enter into pastoral ministry. They will guard you against theological heterodoxy."

He had our attention! We sat on the edge of our seats, waiting for this piece of theological gold dust that would both guarantee our course grade and give us a solid foundation for pastoral ministry.

---

4. C. S. Lewis, *Mere Christianity* (London: William Collins, 2016), 136–37.

Introduction

Looking at us intently, Dr. Letham spoke the three words: "Distinct but inseparable."

It's fair to say that the class was underwhelmed. We had expected something far more profound, more radical, but as the years have gone by, I've become convinced that Dr. Letham was absolutely right.

I quickly realized that the phrase was not original to him. It was first formulated by fourth-century theologian Augustine as he sought to articulate an orthodox understanding of the Trinity. It was picked up again in the fifth century by the Council of Chalcedon as it sought to explain the relationship between Christ's human nature and his divine nature. A question began to form in my mind: Was it a mere coincidence that the phrase used to describe the nature of God as Trinity was also used to describe the union of natures that lies at the heart of the incarnation? I quickly realized that it wasn't.

Humanity was created in the image of God (see Gen. 1:26). As we shall see, this is an intensely relational concept with implications both for our vertical relationship with God and for our horizontal relationships with one another. Dutch Reformed theologian Herman Bavinck wrote, "The Trinity reveals God to us as the fullness of being, the true life, eternal beauty. In God . . . there is unity in diversity, and diversity in unity."[5]

"Unity in diversity, and diversity in unity" is the template for all other relationships in the universe. Contrary to our instincts, unity is founded not on homogeneity—parties being identical—but rather on a union of diverse parties. Human sin has corrupted the unity in diversity that should be present throughout God's creation, and the good news of the gospel is that God has restored this unity in diversity. Accordingly, the phrase "distinct but inseparable" has a crucial role to play in helping us understand who God is, who we are, how we have been redeemed, and where we are heading. That is the focus of this book.

In part 1, we will begin by exploring who God is. We will see that he is one God who has eternally existed in three distinct but inseparable persons. This is what Bavinck meant when he wrote that, in God, there is unity in diversity and diversity in unity. This provides the essential framework

---

5. Herman Bavinck, *Reformed Dogmatics*, ed. John Bolt, trans. John Vriend, vol. 2, *God and Creation* (Grand Rapids: Baker Academic, 2004), 331.

for rightly understanding the unity in diversity that we see in the world around us and the strong desire we have for relationships with people who are unlike us.

In part 2, we will see how the distinct yet inseparable relationship between God and humanity was ruined by the fall. This relationship was restored by God the Son as he assumed a human nature, distinct yet inseparable from his divine nature, which has enabled us to worship God again, distinct yet inseparable from him.

Part 3 looks at the big picture of what God is doing in the world. It walks through the various views of how God relates to the world he has made and shows that the Bible teaches both God's sovereignty and humanity's responsibility. The relationship between these two truths is notoriously tricky to articulate, but I will demonstrate how the language of "distinct but inseparable" provides the necessary framework for understanding God's sovereignty in the world. Moreover, I will show how this doctrine is derived from God's own being, which is both transcendent and immanent.

In part 4, we will consider Christian identity: Who are we as Christians? I will answer this question against the backdrop of current debates about identity. We will see that Christians have both an external, given identity (justification and adoption) and an internal, emerging identity (sanctification). These three gifts of salvation are received distinctly but inseparably through our union with Christ and are therefore both fixed and assured.

Part 5 explores how we grow in the Christian life. It focuses on the ancient yet often forgotten truth that the means of grace (the preaching of the Word and the sacraments) are the spiritual greenhouse of the Christian life. Christians sometimes wonder whether spiritual growth ought to be automatic whenever we use the means of grace. We will see that the phrase "distinct but inseparable" helps us to appreciate how the Holy Spirit uses the means of grace and encourages us to approach them confidently and expectantly.

In the final part of this book, we will seek to apply what we have learned to the church. These are tumultuous times in which the church is being rocked by debates surrounding gender, ethnicity, and identity politics. Many Christians struggle to provide a winsome and plausible response. We will see that the church has always had the conceptual framework to respond faithfully and persuasively to the current challenges—we have just forgotten about it! The distinction without separation that we see within the Godhead and within the gospel is essential to understanding the church. We are one church of many gifts, one church of two genders, and one church of all nations.

I am passionate about this book because I believe its central message is of profound importance to the church today. I ought to acknowledge, though, that it discusses extremely sensitive topics, topics that will touch each of us in different ways. I serve on a church staff where both of my copastors experienced racist bullying at school and where my American colleague lived under the oppression of racial segregation in the United States for many years. My stepmother grew up in an internment camp set up by British colonial authorities to put down the Mau Mau rebellion in Kenya. Though I have not experienced ethnic or sexual discrimination firsthand, I care deeply about it.

The wonderful message of this book is that one day all discrimination will end. As we await that day, we are called to glorify God as his unified, diverse church.

Part 1

Who Is God?

I still remember the first time I asked a Christian to explain the doctrine of the Trinity. I wasn't yet a believer, but I was genuinely interested in learning more. The poor girl looked at me as if I'd asked her how many angels can dance on a pinhead! She replied, somewhat apologetically, "I don't really know. It's one of the mysteries of the Christian faith!" That didn't sound satisfactory to me. If the God who Christians worship is triune, then, surely, there should be something more to say about him than "It's just one big mystery, like in Scooby-Doo!"

During membership classes at City Church, I often ask questions about the theological truths we profess. One of the questions I like to ask is "Why is the doctrine of the Trinity important?" I hear lots of great answers: the doctrine enables God to be love within himself, it shows how he is relational in his very essence, it provides the basis for unity in diversity within the world he has created. All of those things are wonderfully true, and we will discuss them later, but they are consequences of the doctrine of the Trinity, not the doctrine itself. The reason why the doctrine of the Trinity is important—the fundamental reason—is that it describes who God is.

But how much can we know about God? Is it reasonable to think that we can explain the Trinity? Surely the girl was right to say that the nature of God is a mystery. He is infinite, after all, and we are finite. Isn't it ridiculous to imagine that we can understand him?

Now is the time to consider two words that describe the different degrees to which we know things. The first word is "comprehension." To comprehend something is to know absolutely everything there is to know about it. In truth, human beings do not comprehend *anything.*

The second way in which we know things is through "apprehension." We apprehend something when we know true things about it without knowing it exhaustively. I spent seven years teaching commercial law at university. During that time, I apprehended commercial law—that is to say, I knew lots of true things about the subject without knowing it exhaustively. Did my lack of exhaustive knowledge exclude me from teaching? Of course not!

All knowledge of commercial law
Comprehension

Commercial law

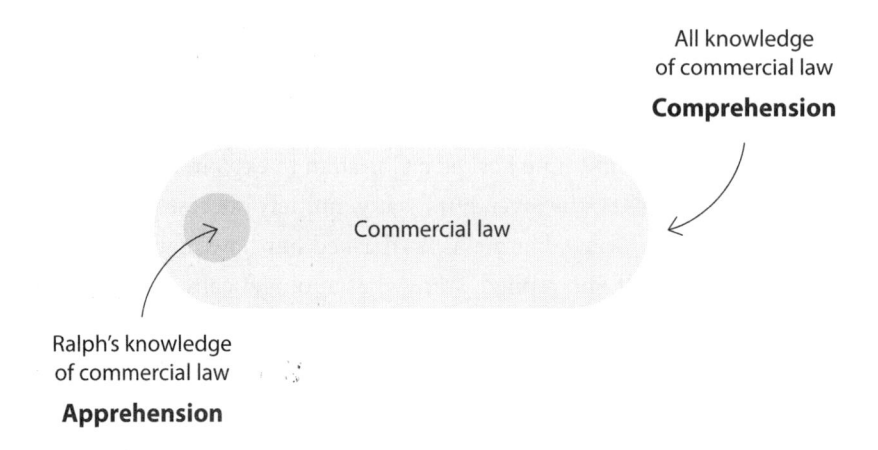

Ralph's knowledge of commercial law
Apprehension

Fig. 1.1. Degrees of Knowing

Some argue that we cannot *truly* know God because we cannot know him exhaustively. But that is flawed logic. There are lots of things about which we have real, true knowledge but not exhaustive knowledge. In fact, that is the way we relate to the vast majority of things in our world, including our job, our parents, our spouse, and our children. We know them and want to know them better, even though we cannot know them exhaustively.

With this in mind—and acknowledging that we cannot know everything there is to know about the Trinity—we will examine what we do know about the Trinity in chapter 1.

1

ONE GOD IN THREE PERSONS

> *The God of the Bible is one God who has eternally existed as three persons. Ultimate beauty is found in the God who is three in one.*

The Bible's teaching on the doctrine of the Trinity can be summarized by three key statements:

1. God is one.
2. God has eternally existed in three persons.
3. Each person of the Trinity is fully God.

God Is One

The Bible repeatedly declares that there is one true God. Deuteronomy 6:4 reads, "Hear, O Israel: The LORD our God, the LORD is one." The Israelites are then told to impress the commandments of this one true God on their children, talking about them when they sit at home and when they walk along the road, when they go to bed and when they rise (see Deut. 6:7).

This affirmation of faith in the one true God is repeated throughout the Old Testament. In Isaiah 44:6–7, we read, "This is what the LORD says—Israel's King and Redeemer, the LORD Almighty: I am the first and I am the last; apart from me there is no God. Who then is like me? Let him proclaim it."

In the New Testament, the apostle Paul writes, "There is one God and one mediator between God and mankind, the man Christ Jesus" (1 Tim. 2:5).

At first glance, these repeated claims that "the LORD is God and there is no other" may sound horribly exclusive. Contemporary Western society claims to be pluralistic: Hindus have their gods, Muslims have Allah, Jews have Yahweh, Sikhs have Waheguru. Many believe that this acceptance of any and all gods furthers the much-promoted goals of tolerance and inclusivity in our society.

However, we must understand that the multiplicity of gods is what divided the peoples of the ancient Near East. The Moabites worshipped Chemosh, the Ammonites worshipped Milcom, and the Edomites worshipped Qaus. These were territorial gods who, their followers claimed, provided protection in return for sacrifices. The gods were tied to particular people in particular places. They were exclusive.

The God of the Bible is inclusive. Because he is the one true God, he is everyone's God—without exception or qualification. After writing that "there is one God and one mediator between God and mankind, the man Christ Jesus," Paul writes that Jesus "gave himself as a ransom for *all* people" (1 Tim. 2:5, 6). Because God is one, his Savior is a savior for *all* who believe (see Rom. 1:16)—without exception. This is radical inclusivism.

God Has Eternally Existed as Three Persons

Some assume that the doctrine of the Trinity is taught only in the New Testament or, even worse, that it was invented by the Council of Nicaea in the fourth century AD (this was the famous claim of Dan Brown in *The Da Vinci Code*). That would be shocking if God has indeed eternally existed as Trinity. However, when you dig into the Old Testament, you quickly discover abundant evidence of plurality within God.

We can start in the very first chapter of the Bible. Genesis 1:26 reads, "Then God said, 'Let us make mankind in our image, in our likeness.'" Notice that the verse includes a plural verb ("let us") and a plural pronoun ("our").

What is the significance of this? It's possible that God is using the "royal we," much as the King of England might say, "We are not impressed by your poor taste in music!" The problem is that there are no other examples of the "royal we" in Hebrew literature. Alternatively, God may be speaking with other beings, such as the angels, as he creates, but that would make these other beings cocreators with God—there is no evidence for this elsewhere in the Bible. The third and most plausible option is that this is the earliest evidence of plurality within God.

We see something similar in Isaiah 6. The prophet Isaiah sees the Lord seated on a throne in the temple. Angels are all around him, and we read in verse 8, "Then I heard the voice of the Lord saying, 'Whom shall I send? And who will go for us?'" Note that God uses both singular and plural pronouns here: "Whom shall *I* send?" and "Who will go for *us*?" This is significant evidence of both unity and plurality within God himself.[1]

There are many more Old Testament passages we could examine, but Psalm 110 is probably the best known, not least because Jesus quotes it in Mark 12:36–37. In verse 1 of the psalm, David writes, "The LORD says to my lord: 'Sit at my right hand until I make your enemies a footstool for your feet.'"

The question is, Who is David referring to when he speaks of two lords? It seems clear that the first lord is Yahweh—that's why our English translations capitalize the word LORD. But who is the second lord? David is writing as the king of Israel, and he has no lord other than God. Yet the second lord is clearly distinct from Yahweh and is given a place at Yahweh's right hand, which is suitable only for one who is himself God. Here again is evidence of plurality in God—one who is a son of David yet the Lord of David, as Jesus notes in Mark 12:37.

While God's eternal existence as three persons is visible in the Old Testament, it comes to the fore in the New. At Jesus's baptism, we see God the Holy Spirit descend on Jesus like a dove while the voice of God the Father declares from heaven, "You are my Son, whom I love; with you I am well pleased" (Mark 1:11). All three persons of the Trinity are active.

Some of the most well-known verses in the Bible contain a triadic formula whereby the names of all three persons of the Trinity are invoked. Perhaps the most famous is the Great Commission, in which Jesus commands his

---

1. In Acts 28:25, the apostle Paul connects this verse to the Holy Spirit. John Calvin writes, "God talks with himself in the plural. And here unquestionably he holds a consultation with his eternal Wisdom and his eternal Power—that is with the Son and the Holy Spirit." *Isaiah* (Wheaton, IL: 2000), 64.

disciples to "go and make disciples of all nations, baptizing them in the name of the Father and of the Son and of the Holy Spirit" (Matt. 28:19).

Almost equally well known, and probably repeated more often in church life, is "the grace," or benediction, found at the end of Paul's second letter to the Corinthians: "May the grace of the Lord Jesus Christ, and the love of God, and the fellowship of the Holy Spirit be with you all" (2 Cor. 13:14). Each of these verses invokes the names of all three persons of the Trinity.

Each Person of the Trinity Is Fully God

The third truth that the Bible teaches is that each person of the Trinity —Father, Son, and Holy Spirit—is fully God. This was challenged in the third and fourth centuries by a theologian named Arius, who argued that the Son had a beginning and, therefore, that there was a time when he did not exist. As such, he saw the Son as the highest of all created beings (an angel) but not God himself. The church condemned this view as inconsistent with Scripture and with what the church had taught from its earliest days.

Let's look briefly at the New Testament evidence. Throughout his gospel, Mark records Jesus doing numerous things that only God can do: on his own authority Jesus cast out demons (1:25–26; 3:23–29), forgave sins (2:1–12), calmed a storm (4:35–41), and raised a young girl from the dead (5:21–43). The teachers of the law clearly understood the implication of his actions, asking, "Why does this fellow talk like that? He's blaspheming! Who can forgive sins but God alone?" (Mark 2:7). The crowning moment of Mark's gospel comes in 15:39, when a battle-hardened Roman centurion declares, "Surely this man was the Son of God!"

Likewise, John's gospel is full of claims that Jesus is God, both from Jesus himself and from others. The book opens with the declaration "In the beginning was the Word, and the Word was with God, and the Word was God" (John 1:1). Later, in verse 14, the Word is identified as the one who became flesh: Jesus.

Now, Jehovah's Witnesses (modern-day Arians who deny that Jesus is God) point out that the definite article ("the") is missing at the end of John 1:1, so they translate the verse "In the beginning was the Word, and the Word was with God, and the Word was a god" (New World Translation).

This is a mistake. It is not uncommon for the definite article to be omitted in New Testament Greek, and the reason for doing so here is quite clear. John has just described how the Word was with God (the Father) in the beginning—he thus emphasizes their distinction and their relationship. In the third part of the sentence, he wants to show that the Word is divine but not identical with the Father, and so he drops the definite article. He is saying, "In the beginning was the Word, and the Word was with [the] God the Father, and the Word was God." In so doing, he shows that the Word is distinct from the Father and yet equally God.

There are numerous confirmations of Jesus's deity throughout John's gospel. For example, there are seven "I am" statements: Jesus says, "I am the bread of life" (6:35), "I am the light of the world" (8:12), "I am the gate" (10:7), "I am the good shepherd" (10:11, 14), "I am the resurrection and the life" (11:25), "I am the way and the truth and the life" (14:6), and "I am the true vine" (15:1). These were incredibly provocative sayings because, in Exodus 3:14, God identified himself to Moses as "I AM WHO I AM." From that point on, this phrase became a way to relate with God personally and to say that God is the same today, yesterday, and forever. By using the phrase so often, Jesus unequivocally identified himself as God. His Jewish listeners certainly understood it that way, as it led them to pick up stones in order to stone him (see John 8:59).

In John's gospel, Jesus is charged with "making himself equal with God" (5:18) and claiming to be God (see 10:33). In his High Priestly Prayer, Jesus declares, "And now, Father, glorify me in your presence with the glory I had with you before the world began" (17:5). The climax of John's gospel comes when Jesus invites Thomas to touch his hands and his side, after which Thomas exclaims, "My Lord and my God!" (20:28).

In addition to the evidence for the Son's deity in the gospel accounts, there are numerous texts that affirm his deity elsewhere in the New Testament. In Romans 9:5, the apostle Paul expressly identifies Jesus as "God over all, forever praised!" and in Titus 2:13, he describes Jesus as "our great God and Savior." The author of Hebrews identifies Jesus as God when he applies Psalm 45:6 to him: "Your throne, O God, will last for ever and ever" (Heb. 1:8), and Peter does something similar when he applies Isaiah 8:12–13 to Jesus in 1 Peter 3:14–15.

The deity of the Holy Spirit is assumed throughout the Bible but made explicit in a number of places. The triadic formulas that we have examined place the Son and the Holy Spirit alongside God the Father. It would be absurd to baptize people in the name of the Son and the Spirit if the Son and the Spirit were somehow of a lower order than God the Father. People would simply be baptized in the name of the Father, as he alone would be God.

Perhaps the most significant passage for establishing the full deity and personhood of the Holy Spirit is Acts 5:1–11. It is a sad and sordid tale. Having seen believers in Jerusalem sell their property and give the proceeds to the poor, Ananias and Sapphira feel (presumably out of a desire to keep up with the Joneses) that they ought to do the same. But their hearts aren't really in it. They want to be seen as generous, but they're not willing to give away everything they receive. So they sell a piece of property but hold back some of the money, giving the rest to the apostles while claiming that they gave it all (see Acts 5:2). The apostle Peter's response is significant: "Ananias, how is it that Satan has so filled your heart that you have lied to the Holy Spirit and have kept for yourself some of the money you received for the land?" (5:3).

Peter continues, "What made you think of doing such a thing? You have not lied just to human beings but to God" (5:4). Do you see what Peter has done? He has explicitly identified the Holy Spirit as God. As nineteenth-century American theologian W. G. T. Shedd put it, "The whole undivided divine nature is in each divine person simultaneously and eternally."[2]

Living It Out: We Worship God as Three in One

Understanding that God is Trinity shapes the way we worship him. No one has put this better than Gregory of Nazianzus, who wrote, "No sooner do I conceive of the one than I am illumined by the splendour of the three; no sooner do I distinguish them than I am carried back to the one."[3] As we worship, we should honor God in his triunity—as both the one and the three. Our reflection on the three should move us to the one and then back

---

2. W. G. T. Shedd, *Dogmatic Theology* (Minneapolis: Klock & Klock, 1979), 1:278.
3. Gregory of Nazianzus, *On God and Christ*, Oration 40.41. Quoted in Robert Letham, *The Holy Trinity: In Scripture, History, Theology, and Worship* (Phillipsburg, NJ: P&R Publishing, 2004), 418.

to the three and then back to the one. This means that it is right and proper to worship each person of the Trinity as well as the whole Trinity.

Some resist this idea and suggest that the Holy Spirit is the "shy member" of the Trinity, who always deflects attention away from himself. It is true that the Holy Spirit glorifies Jesus (see John 16:14) and that the ordinary pattern of prayer in Scripture is to pray to the Father, through the Son and by the Holy Spirit (see Eph. 2:18). Nevertheless, the Spirit remains fully God and worthy of our praise and worship. As John Owen writes, "The Holy Spirit is an eternally existing divine substance, the author of divine operation and the object of divine and religious worship."[4] We worship God as three in one. The most beautiful and supreme Being is one and many—unity in diversity.

Making It Personal

1. How could a deeper understanding of God as Trinity impact who you share the gospel with and how you share the gospel?
2. How should God's eternal existence as three persons affect the way that you pray?
3. Which person of the Trinity do you cry out to most readily, and why? How could a deeper exploration of this question affect your intimacy with God?
4. Take time to pray to the triune God.

---

4. John Owen, *The Works of John Owen*, ed. William H. Goold, vol. 2, *Communion with God* (London: Banner of Truth, 1966), 400.

2

THE RELATIONAL TRINITY

> *Relationship lies at the heart of the universe because God is personal and relational within himself. This explains and shapes our desire for relationship with others.*

In chapter 1, we saw that God has eternally existed as one God in three persons who are each fully God. This necessarily shapes our worship, prayer, and evangelism. In this chapter, we will examine the nature of the persons of the Trinity as well as how the persons relate to one another.

The Persons of the Trinity Are Personal

In Acts 5:3, we read that Ananias lied to the Holy Spirit. People sometimes speak of the Holy Spirit as if he were a force. They say "it" rather than "him." This is understandable—we tend to think of the Spirit as immaterial, and the Spirit is often used to describe God's power in the Old Testament (see Gen. 1:2; Isa. 63:7–14). But you cannot lie to a thing. You cannot lie to a power. I can say all manner of nonsense to a teddy bear or the wind, but I am not lying to it. You lie to persons. Lying is an intensely personal sin that breaches the duty you owe to another person. And Ananias has lied to the Holy Spirit.

But what does it mean to say that the Father, the Son, and the Holy Spirit are *persons*? That is a complex philosophical question that we can only begin to answer here. Suffice it to say that only a person can think, plan, love, speak, send, receive, know, and so on. Persons relate to one another in a personal way—and throughout Scripture, we see the three persons of the Trinity doing just that, even before time itself began.

The High Priestly Prayer in John 17 makes some startling claims about the Son's relationship with the Father before the foundation of the world. Jesus declares, "And now, Father, glorify me in your presence with the glory I had with you before the world began" (John 17:5). A little later in the prayer, he says, "Father, I want those you have given me to be with me where I am, and to see my glory, the glory you have given me because you loved me before the creation of the world" (17:24). Before the universe was created, the Father and the Son shared a mutually glorifying existence, and the Father loved the Son. In other words, the persons of the Trinity have acted personally since before the world began.

In Ephesians 1:4, we read that the Father "chose us in him [Christ] before the creation of the world to be holy and blameless in his sight." The Father eternally foreknew that he would accomplish this by sending his Son to be a sacrificial lamb without blemish (see 1 Peter 1:19–20), thus fulfilling his promise "before the beginning of time" (Titus 1:2). So in eternity we see God the Father glorifying, loving, choosing, knowing, and promising—all personal actions.

This continues throughout the pages of Scripture. The God of the Bible is a covenant God who makes promises to his people. He promises Abraham that he will give him a land, innumerable descendants, and the blessing of his presence forever (see Gen. 12:1–3; 15:1–5; 17:1–8). He is a God who loves, which he proved most powerfully by giving his Son as an atoning sacrifice for sin (see 1 John 4:10). He is a God who sends Moses to Pharaoh (see Ex. 3:10), Nathan to David (see 2 Sam. 12:1), Jonah to Nineveh (see Jonah 1:2), and, ultimately, Jesus into the world (see John 3:16). He is a God who speaks and a God who acts.

As we have seen, the Scriptures present the Holy Spirit as a personal being, not an impersonal force. He can be lied to (see Acts 5:3), he prays on behalf of believers (see Rom. 8:26–27), he speaks (see Acts 13:2), he knows the thoughts of God (see 1 Cor. 2:11), and he gives gifts to Christians (see 1 Cor. 12:4–11). All three persons of the Trinity are personal.

This is so important. What we perceive to be the most fundamental building block of our existence, of our reality, dictates how we see the world around us and how we understand its purpose. Thales, a philosopher in the sixth century BC, believed that everything originated from water—the most basic substance. In his cosmology, Earth solidified from water and now floats on water as a disc. For the New Atheists (people like Richard Dawkins and Sam Harris), the most basic substance is an event: the Big Bang. All observable phenomena derive from this chance event. Both views are deeply impersonal and deny purpose and design.

The Bible offers a very different account of our origins. Before anything else existed, there was God—our fundamentally personal God. Nothing existed before God, and God cannot be stripped down to more basic constituent parts, like atoms or molecules. He is original, the Being from whom everything else comes. And he is personal. That has massive implications for the way we view the world, and we will address these soon.

Misconceptions about How the Persons of the Trinity Relate

Before we get there, let's think more about what it means for God to be personal. He is personal, but he is not *a* person. Rather, as we saw above, he is three persons: Father, Son, and Holy Spirit. It is imperative that we grasp how the three persons relate, and there are two significant traps we need to avoid.

The first trap views the Son and the Spirit as derived from and somehow separate from the Father. This separation is the heresy of tritheism, where the three persons of the Trinity are seen as three separate gods who come together as a divine association to serve a common purpose. This view has more in common with the pantheon of gods in Greek mythology than with the God of the Bible. Nevertheless, it gained influence, especially in the early centuries of the church among Christians on Arabian trade routes, which probably explains why the Qur'an equates Trinitarianism with tritheism.[1] As we have seen, the God of the Bible is one. That means that the Father, the Son, and the Holy Spirit have eternally existed, inseparably unified as one Being.

---

1. Qur'an 4:171; 5:73.

Who Is God?

The second trap we need to avoid is the opposite error. This error was prevalent in the early church—presumably because of the church's determination to avoid tritheism—and it mixed the three persons of the Trinity. Its worst form was the heresy of modalism, the belief that God is one person who has appeared throughout history in three different modes: the Father in the Old Testament, the Son in the New Testament, and the Spirit in the church.

Superficially, this view is appealing, as it seems to simplify the doctrine of the Trinity and help people to understand it. But, in reality, it horribly disfigures God, reducing him to an impersonal, changeable being. It fails to maintain the distinctiveness and integrity of each of the persons of the Trinity, which in turn means that each of them could not truly be a complete person. Moreover, different modes of the same being could not have a personal relationship with one another. I was once a student, I was later a lecturer, and now I serve as a pastor. But in no meaningful sense does my student self personally relate to my lecturer self or my pastor self. That is just nonsense.

It is worth pausing for a moment to note that every analogy Christians use to illustrate the Trinity falls into one of these two traps. Well-meaning youth group leaders often use H_2O as a picture of the Trinity, where the Father is ice, the Son is water, and the Spirit is steam.

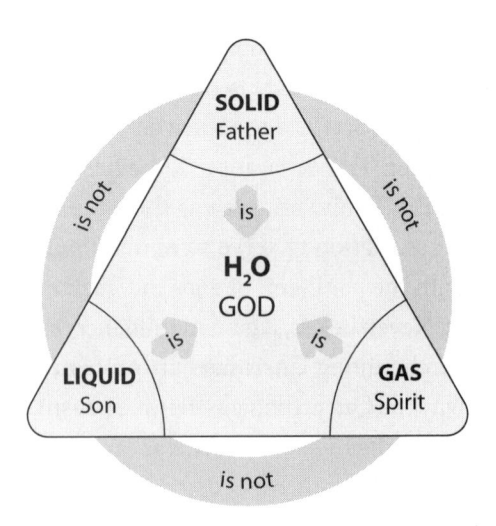

Fig. 2.1. A Modal Misunderstanding of the Trinity

But that is classic modalism: H_2O has three modes of being, and, according to the analogy, so does God. Another popular analogy is that of an egg. A preacher, desperate to present a relatable illustration to his congregation, might say that God is like an egg—the shell is the Father, the white is the Son, and the yoke is the Holy Spirit. But those three parts are separate. The three parts of an egg illustrate tritheism, not the Trinity.

All human analogies for the Trinity fall into either tritheism or modalism. This has always been the case, and it was noted as early as the fourth century by Gregory of Nazianzus: "In a word, there is nothing to satisfy my mind when I try to illustrate the mental picture I have, except gratefully taking part of the image and discarding the rest. So, in the end, I resolved that it was best to say 'goodbye' to images and shadows, deceptive and utterly inadequate as they are to express the reality."[2]

Living It Out: Relationship Is at the Heart of the Universe

Although illustrations fail us, we have seen that the most basic, foundational reality is a personal God who has eternally been in relationship within himself. Before the world began, the Father and the Son were with each other (see John 1:1), they shared their glory (see 17:5), and they loved each other (see 17:26). This is crucial for two reasons.

First, it means that God is personal and relational within himself. He did not need to create the universe in order to have someone to keep him company or to bring him glory. He already had perfectly loving, fulfilling, and glorifying relationships before he created anything. He does not need us (see Acts 17:25). This distinguishes Christianity from all alternative worldviews.

Muslims, for example, claim to believe in a god of love, but if the god they believe in is really a monad (eternally alone), then it is impossible for him to be eternally loving. What do I mean? Well, love requires both a lover and a beloved. The doctrine of the Trinity provides that—three persons who love and are loved eternally. If, however, you believe in a god who has no distinction within himself, then he cannot be eternally loving. Rather,

---

2. Gregory of Nazianzus, "Theological Oration 31," trans. Frederick Williams, *On God and Christ: The Five Theological Orations and Two Letters to Cledonius* (London: SPCK, 2002), 143.

this monadic god only has the potential for love, a potential that would be realized only when he creates a world to love—which, of course, would make him dependent on his creation.

The Trinitarian understanding of God tells us that God is eternally loving within himself and that the love he lavishes on creation is simply a glorious, extravagant overflowing of that love. Thus, the Trinitarian God is in no way dependent on his creation. This is enormously liberating. God does not depend on us to actualize his personal, relational nature. Rather, he invites us to participate in the relationship he already has within himself.

The second reason God's relational nature is vitally important is that it explains our own relational desire. Genesis 1:26 tells us that we were made in the image and likeness of God. This means that we were made for relationship: with God (see 1:26), with one another (see 1:27), and with the world around us (see 1:28). We were made to be loved and to love others. That, fundamentally, is who we are as human beings. It has been ruined by the fall, which is the topic of chapter 4, but for now, it explains why loneliness is such a pervasive and terrible experience. We were made for relationship; we were made for love; but sin has disrupted all of our relationships.

We sometimes think there is something wrong with us if we feel lonely. Actually, the opposite is true. This side of the fall, with all the damage that sin has brought to relationships, there would be something wrong with us if we never felt lonely. We were made for something better—for perfect, loving relationship.

Furthermore, we were made for relationship with people who are different from us in terms of gender, ethnicity, gifting, temperament, and so on. Ira Levin's novel *The Stepford Wives* tells the story of a group of men from Stepford, Connecticut, who decided to turn their wives into robots so that they would be more compliant. Instead of questioning their husbands, the wives now replied, "Yes, dear. Whatever you want, dear!" The problem, of course, was that such a relationship is deeply unsatisfying. We were made for relationship with people who are different from us—people who can engage with us and be distinguished from us. It is only within such a diverse and differentiated relationship that we can find the relational joy and satisfaction that we desire.

We experience a foretaste of this relational joy and satisfaction in the church. The New Testament uses a variety of metaphors to describe the church:

a family, a body, a business, a building. The point is that the church is both one and many and that she glorifies God as her diverse members work together in complementary harmony. In this way, reconciliation and relationship lie at the heart of the church's purpose in the world.

Indeed, in his letter to the church in Ephesus, the apostle Paul insisted that God's manifold wisdom is made known to the heavenly realms as Jew and Gentile are reconciled within the church (see Eph. 3:10). In other words, as believers enjoy relationships across traditional ethnic, social, and cultural lines, God's glory is revealed.

Such reconciliation is made possible only by the gospel, which creates "one new humanity out of the two" (Eph. 2:15), and it can be maintained only by the gospel, which teaches us to value others above ourselves (see Phil. 2:3) and to forgive without limit (see Matt. 18:21–22; Col. 3:12–14). Only the gospel can take groups that have traditionally opposed one another and cause them to flourish through mutually fulfilling relationship. Indeed, in such a gospel-shaped community, we receive a foretaste of the relational joy and satisfaction for which we were created.

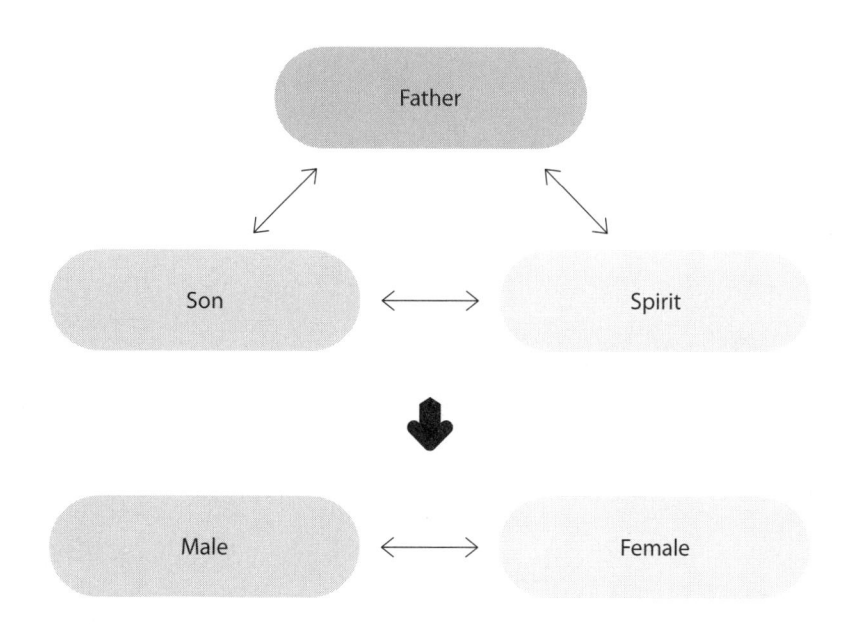

Fig. 2.2. The Eternally Relational Trinity Creates Relational Humanity

Making It Personal

1. Why does it matter that God is personal? If he were impersonal—a force, an essence, a higher power—how would that change the way you relate to him?
2. Which other worldviews include a personal deity or deities? How do they differ from Christianity?
3. Why does it matter that God is inherently and eternally relational?
4. How could a deeper understanding of God's loving and relational nature affect the way we approach relationships?
5. If you are studying this book in a group, discuss how you plan to develop your relationships with God and others.

3

THE DISTINCT BUT INSEPARABLE TRINITY

> *The God of the Bible is one God in three persons, distinct but inseparable. This is why unity in diversity is written into the fabric of the universe.*

In the previous chapter, we saw that the analogies of H_2O or an egg fail to adequately describe the Trinity. In fact, each one teaches something false about the triune nature of God. How, then, should we explain the Trinity to new Christians or to children?

It is here that the phrase on which this whole book is based comes to the fore: the three persons of the Trinity are "distinct but inseparable." As the great fourth-century theologian Augustine wrote, there is "a distinction of persons, and an inseparableness of operation."[1] His emphasis on the distinction of the persons guards against modalism, while his emphasis on their inseparability in action guards against tritheism.

---

1. Augustine, *Nicene and Post-Nicene Fathers: Series I*, ed. Philip Schaff, vol. 6, *Sermon on the Mount, Harmony of the Gospels, Homilies on the Gospels* (London: T&T Clark, 1980), 262.

We Don't Need Balance

We're often told we need to balance different priorities in our lives, such as work and leisure. In the "worship wars" that dominated the church in the late twentieth century, we were told that we needed to balance Word and Spirit.

This talk of balancing priorities or propositions has its roots in eighteenth-century philosophy, particularly in the work of Immanuel Kant and G. W. F. Hegel. These men proposed a philosophical method whereby a proposition, a thesis, is put forward and then countered by an opposing proposition, an antithesis. The resultant tension is resolved by a synthesis—a combination or midway point between the two.

Although this method (called the *dialectical method*) might work in philosophy, it certainly does not work in theology, where, in many cases, two absolute truths must be held together, not merely balanced. We worship God "in the Spirit and in truth," not in something between the two (John 4:24). God is one and three, not a synthesis of those numbers—which, presumably, would make him two! God eternally exists in one being, or one essence, and is three distinct but inseparable persons.

The Persons of the Trinity as Distinct but Inseparable

Let's tease out what distinction without separation looks like within the Trinity. Remember how Augustine put it: the three persons of the Trinity are inseparable in their operation—that is, in their actions or works. The early church father Gregory of Nyssa agreed: "The word Godhead [oneness] is not significant of nature but of operation . . . in the case of the Divine nature we do not . . . learn that the Father does anything by Himself in which the Son does not work conjointly, or again that the Son has any special operation apart from the Holy Spirit."[2] The three persons of the Trinity always work together—inseparably and in unison.

We see this right from the opening verses of the Bible:

---

2. Gregory of Nyssa, *Not Three Gods*, in *Nicene and Post-Nicene Fathers: Series II*, ed. Philip Schaff, vol. 5, *Gregory of Nyssa: Dogmatic Treatises; Selected Writings and Letters* (London: T&T Clark, 1980), 334.

> In the beginning God created the heavens and the earth. Now the earth was formless and empty, darkness was over the surface of the deep, and the Spirit of God was hovering over the waters. And God said, "Let there be light," and there was light. (Gen. 1:1–3)

In context, "God" refers to God the Father (as we saw in our discussion of John 1:1 in chapter 1). The life-giving Holy Spirit hovers over the dark, wet, lifeless surface of the universe (see Gen. 1:2). And God the Son is present as the Father speaks. John 1:2–3 tells us that this creative word is none other than the Son of God—the Word who would become flesh (see John 1:14).

The persons of the Trinity work together inseparably at all points in redemptive history. God the Son is sent by the Father and conceived in human flesh by the Holy Spirit. At Jesus's baptism, the Holy Spirit descends on him like a dove as God the Father speaks from heaven: "You are my son, whom I love; with you I am well pleased" (Mark 1:11).

Even at the resurrection, all three persons of the Trinity are involved. Peter tells us in his Pentecost sermon that God (meaning God the Father) raised Jesus from the dead (see Acts 2:24). The apostle Paul agrees, writing in Romans 6:4 that Christ was raised from the dead "through the glory of the Father." However, later in the same letter, Paul writes that the Holy Spirit raised Jesus from the dead (see Rom. 8:11). All three persons of the Trinity participated.

Augustine anticipated that some may object to this view, arguing that Jesus performed certain miracles that the Father did not. He replied using Jesus's own words: "Where then is that saying, 'The Father who dwelleth in Me, He doeth the works?' (John 14:10)."[3] In everything God does, all three persons of the Trinity are active. They are inseparable in their operation.

This does not, however, mean that the persons of the Trinity are doing exactly the same thing as they work together. They most definitely are not. As Augustine noted, the Father was not born of the virgin, he did not die on the cross, and he did not rise from the dead.[4] The persons of the Trinity remain distinct even as they operate together. They do not mix or intermingle like tea and water. Moreover, this distinction means that the three persons act in different ways.

---

3. Augustine, *Nicene and Post-Nicene Fathers*, 6:262.
4. Augustine, 6:262.

W. G. T. Shedd put it well in his *Dogmatic Theology*: "God the Father and God the Son are so distinct from each other that some actions which can be ascribed to the one cannot be ascribed to the other. The Father 'sends' the Son; this act of sending the Son cannot be attributed to the Son. The Father 'loves' the Son; this act of loving the Son cannot be ascribed to the Son."[5]

Father, Son, and Holy Spirit are one. They are united in being, essence, purpose, and will. Yet they remain distinct as three persons. Indeed, their distinct personhood directs the way they relate with one another and with the world they created. The Godhead—the most basic, irreducible, foundational reality—is both one and many, united and diverse, personal and supreme, distinct and inseparable.

Equal Does Not Mean Identical

We have seen that each person of the Trinity is fully God, and yet they are not identical. They are distinct persons who operate inseparably but differently. As the Reformer John Calvin wrote, "In each [person] the whole divine nature is understood, with this qualification—that to each belongs his own peculiar quality."[6]

We live in a culture that confuses being equal with being identical. Many assume that if two people are to be equal, then they can and should be able to do exactly the same things. This understanding of equality is turned on its head by the Trinity. The three persons of the Trinity are equally and fully God within themselves, they operate inseparably in all things, and yet, in all their actions, they work distinctively according to their peculiar quality as Father, Son, and Holy Spirit.

Our culture says, "You are what you do"—you find your identity in being a banker or a garbage collector, a parent or an orphan. The Bible says the opposite: "You do what you are." The Son is sent and the Spirit empowers because of who they are, ontologically, as the divine Son and Spirit.

As humans, we bring flourishing and order (see Gen. 1:28) in the particular sphere of activity to which God has called us, not to find our identity but

---

5. W. G. T. Shedd, *Dogmatic Theology* (Minneapolis: Klock & Klock, 1979), 1:279.
6. John Calvin, *Institutes of the Christian Religion*, ed. John T. McNeill, trans. Ford Lewis Battles (Philadelphia: Westminster John Knox Press, 1960), 1.18.19.

to live out our identity as God's image bearers. Now, that will look different for each and every one of us. We must resist our culture's insistence that we find our dignity and identity in what we do. There is just as much dignity in being a cleaner as there is in being a doctor. A stay-at-home dad has just as much worth as a senator or a judge. Each display the image of God as they bring order and flourishing to their vocations.

Unity is not found in everyone doing the same thing. God has made us different and has called us to different roles as we work together for the common good. We must champion this and insist that dignity and worth are found in who we are, not in what we do.

Living It Out: Unity in Diversity Is Written into the Fabric of the Universe

The nature of God shows us that unity in diversity is written into the very fabric of the universe. As Irwyn Ince Jr. puts it, "God as Trinity—unity in diversity, diversity in unity—is the heartbeat of the Christian faith."[7] Historically, philosophers have debated whether the universe is fundamentally a static unity or an ever-changing flux. The philosopher Parmenides, for example, championed the former view, arguing that nothing changes in reality and that only our perception changes. Heraclitus took the opposite view, contending that everything changes all the time and that life itself is cyclical.[8]

Most worldviews today emerge from one of these two starting points. Islam, which literally means "submission," emphasizes unity. Everything is expected to conform and submit to the will of Allah, which has a homogenizing effect on Islamic culture. Islamic communities around the world have maintained a large degree of uniformity in language, dress, architecture, and even music, regardless of the geographical location or prevailing culture of the surrounding area. We see the opposite in postmodernism, where the existence of a unifying metanarrative (a big story) is denied. This has profound effects

---

7. Irwyn L. Ince Jr., *The Beautiful Community: Unity, Diversity, and the Church at Its Best* (Downers Grove, IL: IVP, 2020), 37.

8. See the excellent discussion in Christopher Watkin, *Thinking through Creation: Genesis 1 and 2 as Tools of Cultural Critique* (Phillipsburg, NJ: P&R Publishing, 2017), 33.

on postmodern thinking, art, and culture, where the absence of conformity, order, and meaning are prized.

Only a Trinitarian worldview provides a solid foundation for unity in diversity. This is because, as Cornelius Van Til explained, "unity in God is no more fundamental than diversity, and diversity in God is no more fundamental than unity."[9] The Trinity brings together the one and the many and gives them equal precedence. This, in turn, lays the foundation for the unity in diversity that we see in the world around us.

Indeed, it is astounding how ordered yet diverse our universe is. Scientists estimate that there are 400 billion stars in our galaxy and 170 billion other galaxies. Each star and each galaxy are different, yet they share the same features and act consistently. There are over 10,000 species of bird in the sky and more than 32,000 species of fish in the sea. Each is different, and yet there is commonality and consistency among them. The English language has approximately 470,000 words—each is different, and yet grammatical structures and conventions enable them to be brought together in a meaningful way.

The things we most appreciate in the world around us bring together unity and diversity. The best films, music, architecture, literature, even the best cooking, combine order and variety, predictability and surprise.[10] That is because the world we inhabit was created by a God who is one and many, distinct but inseparable.

Making It Personal

1. What in this chapter has deepened your understanding of God's nature?
2. How could this deeper understanding inspire you to worship God more fully?
3. When are calls to "balance" unhelpful? Why?

---

9. Cornelius Van Til, *The Defense of the Faith*, 4th ed. (Phillipsburg, NJ: P&R Publishing, 2008), 48.

10. See Watkin, *Thinking through Creation*, 67; Christopher Watkin, *Biblical Critical Theory: How the Bible's Unfolding Story Makes Sense of Modern Life and Culture* (Grand Rapids: Zondervan, 2022) 39–41.

4. "You do what you are; you are not what you do." What does that mean for you? In what ways is it liberating, and how does it help you to enter new seasons of life?
5. In what ways has this chapter deepened your appreciation of unity in diversity? How might that influence your work, relationships, family life, church, and leisure? If you are studying this book in a group, ask the other members of the group how a deeper understanding of unity in diversity will shape your group and what you do together.

Further Reading for Part 1

Letham, Robert. *The Holy Trinity: In Scripture, History, Theology, and Worship.* Revised and expanded edition. Phillipsburg, NJ: P&R Publishing, 2019.

Reeves, Michael. *Delighting in the Trinity: An Introduction to the Christian Faith.* Downers Grove, IL: IVP Academic, 2012.

Swain, Scott R. *The Trinity: An Introduction.* Short Studies in Systematic Theology. Edited by Graham A. Cole and Oren R. Martin. Wheaton, IL: Crossway, 2020.

Watkin, Christopher. *Thinking through Creation: Genesis 1 and 2 as Tools of Cultural Critique.* Phillipsburg, NJ: P&R Publishing, 2017.

Part 2

What Is the Gospel?

What is the gospel? This is a question we ask every time we interview someone for membership at City Church, and we hear a number of different answers. Some say, "It's forgiveness of sins"; others say, "It means we go to heaven, not hell"; still others say, "It's a right standing with God."

Now, all of those are great answers, but they're answers to a different question: "What does the gospel achieve?" The gospel itself simply means "good news"—it's taken from the old English words *gōd* ("good") and *spel* ("news"). First and foremost, the gospel is not what God has given to us but what God has done in time and history through the life, death, and resurrection of Jesus.

When the apostle Paul set out the gospel in his letter to the church in Rome, he described it as "the gospel of God . . . regarding his Son, who as to his earthly life was a descendant of David" (Rom. 1:1, 3). This tells us that the incarnation lies at the heart of the gospel—the good news. The phrase "distinct but inseparable" is fundamentally important in helping us understand the gospel. If we want to truly grasp the gospel, we need to understand what it meant for God the Son to take on a human nature that is distinct yet inseparable from his divine nature. We will examine this by tracing out God's plan of redemption through the lens of distinction without separation, using the familiar categories of creation, fall, redemption, and restoration.

We will see that the fall happened because humanity challenged its distinction from God in creation. This ruptured the universe and separated

God from humanity. God's plan to reunite humanity to himself required him, God the Son, to assume a distinct yet inseparable human nature. This in turn restored our distinct yet inseparable relationship with God and with one another in all our glorious diversity. Indeed, God's plan is to be glorified by the radically diverse yet inseparable people he has created, redeemed, and restored.

4

CREATION AND FALL

> *Humans were created to be distinct from God—to worship their Creator—and yet be inseparable from God. Human sin is an attempt to deny that distinction, and it separates us from the loving presence of God. This in turn disrupts our relationships with one another.*

In order to understand the good news of the gospel, we need to first understand the bad news of the fall—the account of how humanity ruined its relationship with God. For that, we must return to the very beginning of the Bible.

Creation: Distinction without Separation

When God created humanity, he said, "Let us make mankind in our image, in our likeness, so that they may rule over the fish in the sea and the birds in the sky, over the livestock and all the wild animals, and over all the creatures that move along the ground" (Gen. 1:26). Gallons of ink have been spilt on what the "image" and "likeness" of God mean. Do they refer to humans' self-awareness or cognitive functioning? How about our sense of morality or our ability to communicate? None of these explanations seem satisfactory because they each involve attributes that are shared, at least in part, by other creatures.

To understand what the words *image* and *likeness* mean in this context, we do well to consider what they would have meant to the earliest readers of Genesis. In the ancient Near East, it was common to say that a son is in the likeness of his father, not simply because he looks like him (many sons are relieved to look more like their mothers!) but because of his relationship with his father—he is his father's son. Further, a son was said to be in the image of his father because he represented his father in the community. When a prince visited another kingdom, he went as the "image" of the king because he represented his father and came with his full authority.

That is what is going on in Genesis 1. It is all about relationships that flow one into the other. Adam is made in the *likeness* of God because he is made for a relationship *upward* with God himself—like a child to a father. But he is also made in the *image* of God because, as God's representative, he is designed for a relationship *downward* with the world that God has created.[1] Indeed, as we shall see, God intended the relationship between himself and humanity to be one of distinction without separation.

Humanity Distinct from God

Let us look first at distinction. God's command to humanity in Genesis 1:28 is sometimes called the "creation mandate," and it mirrors God's own creative work in Genesis 1. The six days of creation are broken down into two groups of three. The first three tell us how God brought order to the dark, formless void of verse 2: he separated light from darkness (see vv. 3–5), the sky from the sea (see vv. 6–8), and the sea from the land (see vv. 9–10). The next three days tell us how he filled those spaces with lavish abundance: he flung the stars into space (see vv. 14–19), he placed fish in the sea and released birds into the air (see vv. 20–23), and he filled the land with animals (see vv. 24–25). God ordered the universe, and then he filled it; he subdued the world and made it fruitful. And that is what he commands humans to do too: "Be fruitful and increase in number; fill the earth and subdue it" (1:28).

---

1. For a more detailed discussion of this subject, see Peter J. Gentry and Stephen J. Wellum, *Kingdom through Covenant: A Biblical-Theological Understanding of the Covenants* (Wheaton, IL: Crossway, 2012) 184–202.

There is a crucial difference, however. God created the heavens and the earth out of nothing (*ex nihilo*) with a divine word. We simply cultivate and manufacture as we continue his work in the world. This is the difference between the Creator and the created. We are called to be creative—to take the raw materials that God has placed in the world and do something with them—but we are not called to be creators. We cannot create something out of nothing, and we cannot alter the fundamental principles by which the universe operates.

That is why, in Genesis 2:19–20, God brings the animals and the birds to Adam, who then names them. God creates, and Adam orders. He is the world's first zoologist, bringing order and flourishing to the creation. There is a fundamental distinction written into the relationship between God and man. God is Creator; man is created. They are distinct.

Humanity Inseparable from God

Humanity was also created to be inseparable from God. This is confirmed by several features of Genesis 1–2. First, the word *likeness* describes a relationship akin to that between a father and a son. Humanity was made to enjoy a permanent and enduring relationship with God—inseparable from him. We were made to be worshipers—people captivated by God's greatness who can't help but praise him.

Second, the subtle shift in God's name between Genesis 1 and 2 bears out his relational inseparability from the people he had created. Genesis 1 opens thus: "In the beginning God created the heavens and the earth" (v. 1). This is the large-scale (macro) account of creation, and it describes God using the single Hebrew word *Elohim* ("God").

Genesis 2, however, presents a second, complementary account of creation, beginning with "The Lord God made the earth and the heavens" (v. 4). The word order has shifted—instead of "the heavens and the earth," it is "the earth and the heavens." This is the micro account, which focuses on the creation of the earth and humanity's place in it. The name of God also shifts. He is now described as *Yahweh Elohim* (the Lord God). Yahweh is a much more intimate name for God. As we saw in chapter 1, it is the name that God revealed to Moses in Exodus 3:14. It is God's covenant name, which marks out his commitment to be inseparable from the people he created.

The third feature of this passage that confirms the inseparability of God from the people he created is the fact that he placed humanity into a garden in which he himself dwelled (see Gen. 2:8). In Genesis 3:8, we are given a beautiful picture of God's presence with Adam and Eve when we read of him "walking in the garden in the cool of the day."

Eden was a place where God dwelled with humanity, and that is underlined by the details we are given about the garden in Genesis 2. A river flowed out of Eden as a single stream and then split into four branches, which in turn became the four great rivers of the earth (2:10–14). This tells us something fascinating: Eden was on a mountain, as rivers flow down from mountains (this is also confirmed by Ezekiel 28:13–14, which refers to Eden as the "holy mount of God").

Throughout Scripture, God meets with his people on mountain tops. He meets with Abraham on Mount Moriah (see Gen. 22:2), with Moses on Mount Sinai (also known as Mount Horeb; see Ex. 3:1; 19:3), and with Elijah on Mount Sinai (see 1 Kings 19:11). Further, the temple of God—the place where God supremely and regularly met with his people—was built on Mount Zion in Jerusalem. Indeed, Eden was designed to be the very first temple—a garden temple.

This much is clear from the way the imagery of Eden appears in the decorative instructions for both the tabernacle and the temple. The giant lampstand that stood in the tabernacle (and later in the temple) was shaped like a tree, recalling the Tree of Life (see Ex. 25:31–40). The temple itself was decorated with carvings of flowers, palm trees, pomegranates, and cherubim, evoking the beauty and abundance of Eden (see 1 Kings 6:29; 7:18). And the entrance to the Jerusalem temple was on the east side (see Ezek. 43:1), just as the entrance to Eden faced the east (see Gen. 3:24).

God created human beings to be in the most intimate and personal of relationships with him. He dwelt with humanity. Heaven (the dwelling of God) and earth (the dwelling of humanity) were united as God walked with Adam in Eden. And yet they remained distinct. God was the creator, the giver of life; Adam the creature, the giver of worship. That is how the relationship between God and humanity was designed: distinct, in that God remained the object of humanity's worship, yet inseparable, in that we were created to dwell with God forever.

```
                    God the Creator
```

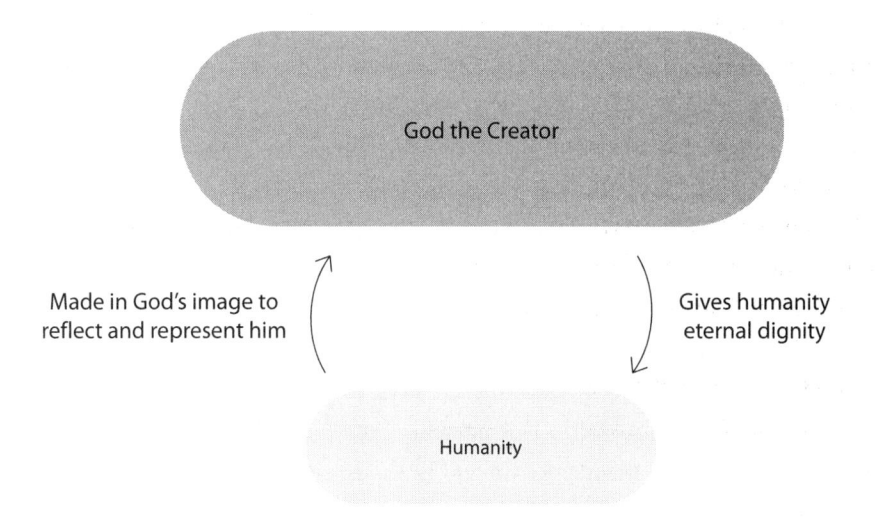

Made in God's image to   Gives humanity
reflect and represent him   eternal dignity

```
                       Humanity
```

Humanity is uniquely like God

Fig. 4.1. God and Humanity—Distinct and Inseparable

The Fall: The Erosion of Distinction Leads to Separation

But everything went wrong at the fall. There is always trouble when things that are designed to be distinct get mixed together—when their distinction is ignored. Consider the parts of a car. The brakes and the steering wheel are designed to be inseparable. Each part contributes something distinct and important to the operation of the car—you are in for a lot of trouble if you try to steer the car with the brakes or stop the car with the steering wheel. Indeed, this will lead to the separation (and likely disintegration) of the car as it crashes into a ditch!

The Erosion of Distinction

Genesis 3 describes how humanity's relationship with God crashed in the most spectacular fashion. In Genesis 2, God gave Adam the owner's manual. He placed him in the garden, let him have a good look around, and then said, "You are free to eat from any tree in the garden; but you must not eat from the tree of the knowledge of good and evil, for when you eat from it you will certainly die" (Gen. 2:16–17). As Ben Cooper has said, God gave humanity "an entire paradise of 'yes,' and just a single tree of 'no.' "[2] That was the owner's manual. You can enjoy anything, absolutely anything at all. Eat, drink, and be merry. Just avoid this one tree.

Notice that God did not give a reason for his command in this passage. We often want reasons, don't we? When I tell my children that they are not to do something, they often ask, "But why?" and my response is, "Because I want the best for you. Trust me!" God's command to Adam in Genesis 2 is an invitation to trust him—to take him at his word. God has created a paradise for Adam to live in, and now he says, as it were, "Trust me. Trust me to be God and to look after this paradise."

Consider what this means. Adam and Eve's decision to follow the serpent rather than God was not a trivial infraction. It was a vote of no confidence in God. It was an attempted de-godding of God. Adam and Eve were saying, in effect, "We don't trust you to be God—to do what's best in the world. We want to be the gods of our own lives."

In fact, that is the very promise with which the serpent tempted Eve in 3:5: "For God knows that when you eat from [the tree] your eyes will be opened, and you will be like God, knowing good and evil." The sin of Genesis 3 was that Adam and Eve sought to usurp God's authority, to blur the lines of distinction between the Creator and the created. They wanted to become God in determining good and evil, right and wrong. Adam and Eve tried to reject distinction in their relationship with God.

The Terrible Separation

This rejection of distinction leads to a terrible separation. God sentences Adam and Eve to death, just as he had warned. But the weird thing is—and it really is puzzling when you read Genesis for the first time—they do not die immediately. In fact, Genesis 5:5 tells us that Adam goes on to live until the ripe old age of 930. What's going on here?

The problem is that we have too narrow a view of death. It is not that the word *die* in Genesis 2 does not mean physical death. It does. But physical

---

2. Barry Cooper and Nate Morgan Locke, *Life Explored Leader's Handbook* (Epsom, UK: The Good Book Company, 2016), 95.

death is merely a symbol or a symptom of a much more significant death, one that happened the moment Adam and Eve ate from the Tree of the Knowledge of Good and Evil.

Let me explain. At the heart of the concept of death lies separation. Consider what happens when a person dies. Their body ceases to function, their heart stops pumping, their brain stops firing neurons; and, according to the Bible, their soul separates from their body. *Physical* death involves a radical separation of soul and body that, the Bible teaches, leaves us "unclothed" (2 Cor. 5:4). But the separation of physical death is only a picture of a far worse separation that took place the very moment Adam and Eve rebelled—the separation of *spiritual* death.

Did you notice what happened in Genesis 3? The God who walked with Adam in the garden "banished him from the Garden" (Gen. 3:23) and placed cherubim and a flaming sword at the entrance to prevent him and his wife from ever returning to the place of God's presence again. It was a terrible separation, and it happened immediately.

Sin separates humans from God

Fig. 4.2. Fallen Humanity—Distinct and Separate

But there is a worse separation to come—that of *eternal* death. This is pictured in Revelation 20, which calls it the "second death" (v. 6), a place of torment, day and night, forever (see v. 10). It is an eternal, spiritual separation from the loving rule of God. That terrible separation is the ultimate sentence for humanity's decision to challenge the divinely ordered distinction between the loving Creator and the worshipful created.

Genesis 3 offers a ray of hope, however. As we have seen, only one of the separations took place immediately—*spiritual* death. Adam and Eve were spared the horrors of *physical* and *eternal* death for a time. This hinted at the possibility of an escape, a way out of eternal death.

The chapter provides two further clues to this hope. The first is what God does when Adam and Eve begin to feel the nakedness and shame of their sin. The Lord took an animal and used its skin to cover them (see Gen. 3:21). An animal died so that humanity's shame could be covered. Second, the Lord makes a promise to the serpent: one of Eve's offspring will crush his head (see Gen. 3:15). This is a pregnant promise (quite literally) that, one day, a man would come to reverse the terrible separation. It points to redemption—the subject of the next chapter.

Living It Out: We Are Valuable and Distinctive Image Bearers

Genesis 1 shows us that humanity is intrinsically and uniquely valuable. This is an unpopular idea today. In 2013, renowned television presenter Sir David Attenborough famously described humans as a "plague on the Earth."[3] Zoologists point out that we share 97 percent of our DNA with chimps. Some argue that there is nothing special about human beings and that we should not hold a lofty view of the dignity and worth of humanity. Australian ethicist Peter Singer goes so far as to say that "the traditional view of the sanctity of human life will collapse under pressure from scientific, technological and demographic developments."[4]

Genesis 1 proves how wrong this view is. The sanctity of human life will not collapse because it is rooted in what God has revealed about the nature and value of humanity. God created man and woman in his image for relationship with him. This gives us a permanent dignity and worth that cannot be violated.

To be sure, the image of God in us has been distorted by the fall—we are marred masterpieces. But the Scriptures are absolutely clear that we remain

---

3. Louise Gray, "David Attenborough – Humans Are Plague on Earth," *The Daily Telegraph*, January 22, 2013, https://www.telegraph.co.uk/news/earth/earthnews/9815862/Humans-are-plague-on-Earth-Attenborough.html.

4. Peter Singer, "The Sanctity of Life," *Foreign Policy*, October 20, 2009, https://foreignpolicy.com/2009/10/20/the-sanctity-of-life/.

in the image of God and are to be afforded the dignity and respect that comes with this. Indeed, in Genesis 9:6, after both the fall and the flood, the Lord confirms that human life should not be taken because humans are made in the image of God. This is a far cry from Singer's claim that humans are no more intrinsically valuable than animals.[5]

As God's distinctive and valuable image bearers, we are called to represent him in the world he has made. This is not simply the calling of an elite group. We tend to see some vocations as more important, spiritual, or honorable than others. For example, we speak about doctors and pastors as "having vocations," while bankers and cleaners simply "do jobs." We admire the creativity of artists and actors but assume that those who stock shelves or answer phones are simply completing mundane and uncreative tasks.

In truth, though, all human beings are called to continue God's creative work. We all have a vocation to bring order and flourishing to the part of the world in which God has placed us. Doctors are called to repair and reset broken bones, to bring order to overactive thyroids and see their patients flourish. Cleaners are called to bring order to a chaotic office at the end of the day so that the workers can return the following morning and flourish in their environment. Teachers are called to bring order and structure to young minds so that their students can be fruitful and flourish in the future. Stay-at-home parents are called to bring order and structure to the family home, that children may grow up in a safe, nurturing environment and that the whole family may flourish in the refuge of home.

All human beings are called to be distinctive image bearers in order to glorify God. And we need one another. Doctors need cleaners to provide an environment in which they can help others heal. Bankers need construction workers to build safe and functional offices out of which they can loan and invest money to help businesses to flourish. Teachers need their stay-at-home spouse to bring order to their homelife and to raise their young children. All human beings are made in the likeness of God, and we need one another in our distinctive callings to bring order and flourishing to our lives together. True unity and flourishing are founded on our distinctive callings as we seek to image God.

---

5. For more on this view, see Peter Singer, *Animal Liberation Now: The Definitive Classic Renewed* (London: Bodley Head, 2023).

Making It Personal

1. How does the inseparability of God from humanity affect our understanding of human dignity and self-identity?
2. What are some of the ways that you see the erosion of distinction between God and humanity celebrated in our culture and in the church today? How does this erosion of distinction seep into your own thinking and heart attitudes?
3. How would you explain death as separation from God to a child? How does the distinction between physical, spiritual, and eternal death help? What illustrations might you use?
4. What would it look like for you to image God in your vocation as you pursue order and flourishing?
5. If you are discussing this book in a group, ask the other members of the group how you might bring order and flourishing to the world.

5

REDEMPTION

> *God the Son has undone the work of the fall by uniting to his divine nature a distinct yet inseparable human nature. God will forever be united to humanity, and this grounds the inherent dignity and worth of every human being in all their glorious diversity.*

In the previous chapter, we saw how God created humanity to be distinct but inseparable from him. The fall struck at the very heart of this relationship. Humanity's attempt to remove the distinction between God and itself ruptured the relationship and threatened eternal separation between the two. The good news of redemption is that God has bridged the gap and restored the distinction by taking on a human nature that is distinct but inseparable from his divine nature.

God Becomes Human

John's gospel starts in the most incredible way. Using the language of Genesis 1, John paints a picture of the Word on a huge canvas. The title "Word" is deliberately evocative, recalling the action of God's word in creation. The Word has been there from the very beginning, John writes; before anything, "the Word was with God" (v. 1). He is the one "through [whom] all things were made" (v. 3) and the one who gives life and light to "all mankind" (v. 4). The Word is none other than God himself—God the Son, distinct but inseparable from the Father and the Holy Spirit.

Later, John tells us that "the Word became flesh and made his dwelling among us" (v. 14). This verse is so familiar to many Christians that we usually let it pass by us. But it is mind-blowing: God became flesh! Let that knock the wind out of you.

Moreover, John could have said that the Word became a man—but he didn't. He deliberately chose the word *flesh*, the Greek word *sarx*, which is a crude term that emphasizes human frailty. The One who flung the stars into space cried for his mother's milk. The Word who upholds the universe put his head down on a pillow to sleep each night. The One who is Light and Life suffered pain and agonizing death. God himself became *in carne*—Latin for "in flesh." C. S. Lewis called it "the grand miracle."[1]

One Person with Two Natures

It is important to clarify what John is not saying in these verses. He is not suggesting that the Word *changed into* flesh and ceased to be God. The second person of the Trinity remained fully God, as we saw in the previous chapter, and continued to uphold the universe according to his divine nature.

Nor is John suggesting that the Word merely *appeared* to be human. That is the mistake that the Docetists (from the Greek word *dokein*, meaning "to seem") made in the first and second centuries. The rest of the New Testament makes it abundantly clear that Jesus is fully human. He was made like us in every way, fully human, and yet without sin (see Heb. 2:17; 4:15). When God the Son assumed human flesh two thousand years ago, he who was fully God became fully man as well. Humanity had been separated from God by the fall, but in his one person, God the Son united humanity to God once more. He became one person with two natures—human and divine —and through that one person he made it possible for sinful humanity to be reconciled to God.

Let's look at the two natures in turn.

---

1. C. S. Lewis, *God in the Dock* (London: HarperCollins, 1971), 48–58.

Fully Human

Why did God the Son have to be fully human? First, he had to represent us as he perfectly obeyed God the Father. As we have seen, Adam disobeyed God and sought to dissolve the distinction between the Creator and the created. When he did that, he did it as our representative. When Neville Chamberlain declared war on Germany on September 3, 1939, he did so as the United Kingdom's representative. It had implications not just for Chamberlain himself but for all the citizens of the United Kingdom.

In the same way, when Adam sinned, he did so as humanity's representative. That means that the terrible separation from God he experienced was not just for him alone but for all of humanity. We need a second Adam, a "last Adam," as 1 Corinthians 15:45 puts it, to represent us in perfectly obeying God.

That is what we see in the gospel accounts. Right at the start of Jesus's public ministry, the Holy Spirit led Jesus into the wilderness to be tempted like Adam.[2] But this was different. Adam was placed in a garden, surrounded by abundance and beauty. He was tempted once, and he fell straightaway. Jesus was sent into a wilderness without food. He was tempted repeatedly and resisted every single time (see Matt. 4:1–11). God the Son became human flesh so that he could perfectly obey God as our representative—undoing the work of Adam.

Second, God the Son became fully human so that he could be our substitute, taking the punishment for sin that we deserve. As you read the Old Testament, you can't miss the blood that drips off its pages. There is chapter after chapter of sacrifice to deal with sin. It begins with the animal sacrificed in Genesis 3 to cover Adam and Eve's shame and continues with the sacrifices of Abel, Noah, and Abraham. The law of Moses sets out detailed provisions for the Passover sacrifice, the sacrifice of atonement, sin offerings, burnt offerings, thank offerings, and much more. It becomes clear that these sacrifices need to be distinct from the sinful people who offer them—otherwise, they could not atone for the sin. The Passover sacrifice had to be a lamb "without defect" (Ex. 12:5) whose bones were not broken

---

2. Luke's account (Luke 4:1–13) undoubtedly parallels Israel's experience as well. Israel was God's son who failed the forty-year wilderness test, while Jesus is God's Son who triumphed in the forty-day wilderness test.

(see Ex. 12:46). It was symbolic. The sacrifice was to be whole and perfect in a way that sinful humanity was not.

The problem with the lambs and goats and bulls, however, was that they were not simply distinct from humanity—they were separate as well, an entirely different species. And as the writer to the Hebrews declares, "it is impossible for the blood of bulls and goats to take away sins" (10:4). Thus, we needed a sacrifice that was distinct from humanity, in that God the Son is sinless, and yet inseparable from humanity, in that he is fully man. Hebrews puts it so clearly: "He had to be made like them, fully human in every way, in order that he might become a merciful and faithful high priest in service to God, and that he might make atonement for the sins of the people" (2:17).

Fully God

So why did our Savior have to be fully God as well? The Bible confirms again and again that salvation is from the Lord (see Pss. 3:8; 62:1; Jonah 2:9). Humanity is powerless to save itself. It is like a swimmer with a lead weight tied around his neck trying to save another swimmer. It is impossible. Every human being is judged and condemned already by their own sin.

And even if it were possible to find a human who had never sinned (which it is not—apart from Jesus), how could that one finite person bear the penalty for the infinite sins of billions of people? None could, which is why the infinite God had to bear the penalty in his human nature. No one has put it better than the seventeenth-century Puritan writer Stephen Charnock:

> [Christ's] sufferings were partly finite, partly infinite. They were finite, in regard of the time of duration; finite in regard of the immediate subject wherein he suffered, his human nature; which being a creature could no more become infinite, than it could become omnipotent, omniscient, or eternal. But in regard of the person who suffered, the sufferings were infinite; the Deity being in conjunction with the humanity. That which is finite in regard of time and in regard of the subject may be infinite in regard of the object.... The sacrifice of Christ deserves an infinite acceptance, because it is offered by an infinite person.[3]

3. Stephen Charnock, *Discourses on Christ Crucified* (Philadelphia: Presbyterian Board of Publication, 1841), 201–2.

In other words, because Christ's infinite divine nature is inseparable from his human nature in his person, Christ's sufferings could pay the infinite price for humanity's sin. God alone could do it, but he could do it only in a human nature.

Distinct but Inseparable

Have you ever heard a preacher try to explain the incarnation? It can be tricky, and people often resort to soundbites in the hope of making things clear. I've heard the incarnation described as "God in a body" or "God coming into the man Christ Jesus." Both descriptions are profoundly flawed. The good news is that these difficulties (and mistakes) are nothing new—in fact, they were resolved more than a thousand years ago. To explain how, I'll introduce you to two Turkish bishops.[4]

Inseparable and Indistinct

The first bishop we need to consider is Apollinarius, a bishop of Laodicea in the fourth century. Apollinarius taught that God the Son merely assumed a human body, not a human mind or a higher soul;[5] rather, his divine nature provided the mind and the higher soul. This was the "God in a body" error, which, on the face of it, might sound harmless. But the early church condemned it, and with good reason.

Gregory of Nazianzus explained, "If anyone has put their trust in a human being lacking a human mind, they are themselves mindless and not worthy of salvation. For, what has not been *assumed* has not been *healed*; it is what is united to his divinity that is saved. . . . Let them not grudge us our total salvation or endue the Saviour with only the bones and nerves and mere appearance of humanity."[6]

Human beings are both body and soul, and sin has ravaged both in their totality. If God only assumed a human body, he only redeemed (healed) the

---

4. As an aside, many assume that the early church was White and Western European, but as we shall see, most of the prominent early church theologians were Eastern or North African.
5. Apollinarius distinguished between the "lower" soul, which is the essence of a living creature, and the "higher" soul, which is the rational mind.
6. Gregory of Nazianzus, Letter 101, in *The Christian Theology Reader*, ed. Alister E. McGrath, 3rd ed. (Oxford: Blackwell Publishing, 2007), 270. Emphasis added.

human body. The mind and the higher soul would remain enslaved and condemned. By emphasizing inseparability but not distinction, Apollinarius ripped the soul out of humanity's redemption.

> God in a Man

God put on a human body

Fig. 5.1. Apollinarianism—Indistinct and Inseparable

Distinct and Separate

The second bishop, Nestorius, lived in Constantinople in the fifth century. He fell into the opposite error. Nestorius spoke of a "conjunction" of natures in Christ rather than a "union," insisting that Christ was both the eternal Son of the Father and the human son of Mary. Nestorius maintained the distinction between Christ's divine and human natures, unlike Apollinarius, but did not recognize their inseparability. In his view, they were like two pieces of sandwich bread stuck together. This is the "God came into the man Christ Jesus" error.

> God   A Man Called Jesus

God joined himself to a man

Fig. 5.2. Nestorianism—Distinct and Separate

Cyril of Alexandria responded, "The natures which were brought together to form a true unity were different; but out of both is one Christ and one Son. We do not mean that the difference of the natures is annihilated by reason of this union; but rather that the divinity and humanity, by their inexpressible and inexplicable concurrence into unity, have produced for us the one Lord and Son Jesus Christ."[7]

In other words, God the Son remains one person, but he has two natures: divine (which he has had eternally) and human (which he assumed at the incarnation). One might ask, Is this really so important? Why worry whether Jesus is two persons or one person with two natures? The answer is that our salvation depends on it. We need a Savior with both a human and a divine nature.

No one has put it better than Archbishop Anselm in his book *Cur Deus Homo* ("Why God Became Man"): "The debt was so great that, while man alone owed it, only God could pay it, so that the same person must be both man and God. Thus it was necessary for God to take manhood into the unity of his person, so that he who in his own nature ought to pay and could not should be in a person who could."[8]

Only the God-man—one person with two distinct but inseparable natures (human and divine)—could save sinful humanity. Therefore, God the Son (who has forever been God, in perfect triune relationship) assumed a human nature at the incarnation.

Distinct but Inseparable

To resolve the problems created by the teachings of Apollinarius and Nestorius, in AD 451 the church convened a council in the city of Chalcedon near modern-day Istanbul. The council composed a statement that sought to guard the doctrine of the incarnation against these errors—it became known as the Chalcedonian Definition:

> We, then, following the Holy Fathers, all with one consent, teach people to confess one and the same Son, our Lord Jesus Christ, the same perfect in Godhead and also perfect in manhood; truly God and truly man, of a reasonable soul and body [against Apollinarianism] . . . one

---

7. Cyril of Alexandria, Letter IV, in *The Christian Theology Reader*, ed. Alister E. McGrath, 3rd ed. (Oxford: Blackwell Publishing, 2007), 276.
8. Anselm, *Why God Became Man*, in *A Scholastic Miscellany: Anselm to Ockham*, ed. Eugene R. Fairweather (Philadelphia: Westminster, 1961), 176.

and the same Christ, Son, Lord, only begotten, to be acknowledged in two natures, unconfusedly, unchangeably, indivisibly, inseparably; the distinction of natures being by no means taken away by the union [against Nestorianism], but rather the properties of each Nature being preserved, and concurring into One Person and One Subsistence.

This is such an important statement. At the incarnation, God the Son assumed a fully human nature—body and soul. He now exists as one person with two distinct natures, divine and human, that are inseparably joined together but not combined or mixed in any way. Only such a Savior could save humanity. Therefore, that is exactly the Savior God gave us!

Living It Out: The Incarnation Changes Everything

The incarnation has so many implications for our lives today. It is the gospel, the means by which we can be saved—there's no greater implication than that. In this section, however, I want to focus on three more implications of the incarnation that we can easily miss or overlook.

Humans Are Valuable from Conception

In the previous chapter, we saw that humans have dignity and worth because we are made in the image of God. We can now add that God confirmed this worth when he chose to unite himself to humanity. When the second person of the Trinity came to dwell on earth, he became a man, not a chimp, a rodent, or a bird. This confirms the unique value and dignity of human life, which must be protected regardless of a person's age, gender, ethnicity, capacity, dependence, or cognitive ability.

The human race has a disturbing history of denying the value and dignity of particular ethnic and religious groups. From Africans in the United States to Jews in Hitler's Germany to Tutsis in Rwanda, human societies have a tragic track record of shunning particular groups and denying their dignity and inviolability. Only a thoroughly biblical understanding of creation (in God's image) and redemption (through the incarnation) can provide a secure foundation for human rights. And only such an understanding can provide the necessary motive and desire for people to pursue unity across ethnic, social, political, and cultural boundaries. After all, as the apostles emphasized, God the Son united himself to the human race, not to some subcategory of humanity.

Interestingly, the fifth-century debates about the two natures of Christ also resolve the thorny question of when human life begins. This determines the treatment of the most vulnerable group in Western society: the unborn. Most societies assume that human life begins not at conception but at some later point (some call this personhood, while others call it ensoulment). This provides the philosophical foundation for permitting abortion on demand during the early weeks of pregnancy. The Chalcedonian Definition, however, shows us that this position is unsustainable.

Let me explain why. Chalcedon's opposition to Nestorianism means that the embryo in Mary's womb did not have an existence independent from God the Son prior to the incarnation. Remember that Christ's divine and human natures are inseparable. Therefore, God the Son assumed human flesh at the point of fertilization. But Chalcedon's opposition to Apollinarianism also means that the human nature assumed by God the Son had to be fully human, body and soul, from the moment he assumed it. He did not assume a potential human nature. Therefore, human life must begin at fertilization and must be intrinsically valuable from that point onward.

Our society teaches that dignity and worth are earned. The Bible teaches that they are ascribed and universal to all human life from the point of conception. This provides a radical basis for unity among God's people because all will be valued in the church. Indeed, in God's economy, those whom the world regards as weak or less honorable (which, in our culture, includes ethnic minorities, the unborn, and the elderly) are to be given great honor (see 1 Cor. 12:22–25).

Particularity Matters

God the Son did not assume humanity in the abstract. He became a particular man—an Israelite, of the tribe of Judah, from the obscure town of Nazareth. Unlike medieval portrayals of him in the West, Jesus had dark hair and olive skin. He was trained by Joseph as a carpenter, and he spoke Aramaic, not English. Jesus lived in an occupied country under Roman rule, and he partook of Mediterranean cuisine, music, and culture. He was a particular human being with a particular gender, race, culture, language, and history. Yet his life, death, and resurrection were for *all* humanity.

This is crucial. We live in a time when distinctions of ethnicity, gender, and culture are either ignored and papered over or else so emphasized that demographic groups are set against one another. The incarnation tells us that particularity matters. God created humanity to image him in its awesome diversity of gender, race, and culture. God the Son assumed a particular human nature, confirming the beauty of our distinctive genders, ethnicities, languages, skin colors, cultures, and personalities. And yet he did so to redeem the whole—so that people from every "nation, tribe, people and language" might gather as one to worship him (Rev. 7:9).

Particularity and diversity matter—they show forth the beauty of the "one" people of God as they gather to worship him. We will return to this in much more detail in part 6, when we look at the church.

God Knows What It Is Like to Be Human

Some people can help us but don't truly understand us. Presidents and prime ministers have immense power to improve their citizens' lives, but they do not know their citizens personally and individually. Other people can understand us but can't help us, like the best friend who provides a shoulder to cry on but can't numb our pain or end our heartbreak. The gods of most religions fall into the former category—they claim to be powerful but remain remote. Jesus Christ has both power and empathy.

In some ways, God has always known what it is like to be human—he is all-knowing (omniscient), after all. But when he took on flesh, God the Son experienced what it was like to be human. He experienced what it is like to mourn (the shortest verse in the Bible, John 11:35, is "Jesus wept"), to be hungry, lonely, shamed, tempted, falsely accused, hated, abandoned, tortured, and killed. Hebrews 4:15 declares, "We do not have a high priest who is unable to empathize with our weaknesses, but we have one who has been tempted in every way, just as we are—yet he did not sin."

When we struggle, when temptation seems overwhelming, when we think that the world has turned its back on us and that we can't carry on—at those very points, Jesus is with us, and he knows exactly how we feel.

As Dane Ortlund wrote, "Our pain never outstrips what he himself shares in. We are never alone. The sorrow that feels so isolating, so unique, was endured by him in the past and is now shouldered by him in the present."[9]

Making It Personal

1. Jesus lived a perfect human life. How does this expand your understanding of the gospel and shape the way you worship him?
2. Why does it matter that Jesus is both fully God and fully man? Which nature do you tend to focus on most when praying?
3. How does God the Son's humanity shape your understanding of God the Father's view of you?
4. What can you do to champion the intrinsic value of all human life?
5. How can you value your own particularity more? What might it look like to celebrate diversity while maintaining unity within the church?

---

9. Dane Ortlund, *Gentle and Lowly: The Heart of Christ for Sinners and Sufferers* (Wheaton, IL: Crossway, 2020), 48.

6

RESTORATION

> *Through his resurrection, God the Son has transformed humanity. He has closed the separation occasioned by the fall and has ensured that resurrected humanity will never fall again.*

Redemption is not an end in itself. We have been freed from slavery to sin and death for a particular purpose—not simply a restoration of creation but something far, far better.

Humans Become God?

In 2011, Israeli author Yuval Noah Harari published the bestselling *Sapiens: A Brief History of Mankind*. In it, Harari sought to trace the history of humanity from the Stone Age to the twenty-first century. His basic argument was that humanity came to dominate the earth because it is the only species that can collaborate in large numbers.

Harari followed up that book in 2015 with *Homo Deus: A Brief History of Tomorrow*, in which he predicted what the future has in store. He begins, "Having secured unprecedented levels of prosperity, health and harmony . . . humanity's next targets are likely to be immortality, happiness and divinity. . . . Having raised humanity above the beastly level of survival struggles, we will now aim to upgrade humans into gods, and turn *Homo sapiens* into

Homo deus.[1] This sounds like something from a Jules Verne novel, but Harari sees it as the future. He believes that humanity will one day replace itself with a physical and mental upgrade—the god-man.[2]

As we have seen, however, humanity's transformation already occurred over two thousand years ago. Jesus Christ is the Homo Deus who came to defeat sin, suffering, Satan, and death, not just for himself but for all who would be united to him by faith. The title for this section—shocking as it is—is taken from one of the most famous works on the incarnation, written by Athanasius, a fourth-century bishop of Alexandria, who wrote, "The Word became man that we might become God."[3]

Now, that can easily be misunderstood, and, indeed, the Eastern church developed it into a full-blown doctrine of deification.[4] But Athanasius was expressing a profoundly biblical idea. In his second letter, the apostle Peter writes,

> His divine power has given us everything we need for a godly life through our knowledge of him who called us by his own glory and goodness. Through these he has given us his very great and precious promises, so that through them you may *participate in the divine nature*, having escaped the corruption in the world caused by evil desires. (2 Peter 1:3–4)

We will return to this passage in part 4 when we look at the Christian life. At this point, however, let us focus on two ways in which Jesus Christ—the God-man—has restored humanity.

Distinct but Inseparable Again

As we have seen, humanity was created to be distinct from God—we are the created rather than the Creator—and yet inseparable from him in

---

1. Yuval Noah Harari, *Homo Deus: A Brief History of Tomorrow* (London: Penguin, 2015), 24.
2. Harari, 410.
3. Athanasius, *On the Incarnation*, §54 in *Nicene and Post-Nicene Fathers: Series II*, ed. Philip Schaff, vol. 4, *Sermon on the Mount, Harmony of the Gospels, Homilies on the Gospels* (Peabody, MA: Hendrickson Publishers Inc, 1995), 65.
4. See Robert Letham, *Through Western Eyes: Eastern Orthodoxy: A Reformed Perspective* (Fearn, UK: Christian Focus, 2010), 243–68.

terms of relationship and dependence. Adam and Eve's attempt to erode this distinction led to the terrible separation of death, in all its forms. In Christ, that separation has been dealt with forever.

First, Jesus has dealt with the separation of body and soul wrought by physical death. As John Owen put it, the cross heralded the death of death in the death of Christ.[5] Jesus died our death in our place so that the separation of soul from body need be only temporary. The Christian can look physical death in the face and say, "Where, O death, is your victory? Where, O death, is your sting?" (1 Cor. 15:55). This is because we look forward to being "clothed instead with our heavenly dwelling, so that what is mortal may be swallowed up by life" (2 Cor. 5:4).

Second, Jesus has dealt with the separation of spiritual death. He has sent the Holy Spirit from heaven to indwell believers and unite them to himself in his humanity. One of the apostle Paul's favorite phrases was "in Christ." He used it more than eighty times across all his letters, including twenty-seven times in Ephesians alone. Christians are now united to Christ—distinct from him but eternally inseparable. God the Son has drawn near to us by assuming humanity so that we can draw near to him by the Holy Spirit. In being united to Christ, we are united to God the Father and God the Holy Spirit. Jesus's prayer has been answered:

> I pray also for those who will believe in me through their message, that all of them may be one, Father, just as you are in me and I am in you. May they also be in us so that the world may believe that you have sent me. I have given them the glory that you gave me, that they may be one as we are one—I in them and you in me—so that they may be brought to complete unity. (John 17:20–23)

Through Christ's work, humans have been caught up into the unity of love and joy that the Trinity experiences.

---

5. John Owen, *The Death of Death in the Death of Christ* (Edinburgh: Banner of Truth, 1959).

Third, Jesus has overcome the separation of eternal death through his resurrection and ascension. When Neil Armstrong set foot on the moon on July 20, 1969, he uttered the now-famous words "That's one small step for man, one giant leap for mankind." The same words can be applied to Jesus's ascension. It was one small step for Jesus—God the Son was simply returning to his heavenly home. Yet it was one giant leap for mankind. Jesus took humanity into heaven—body and soul.

The fall wrenched heaven (the dwelling of God) and earth (the dwelling of humanity) apart. Jesus's life, death, resurrection, and ascension have brought them back together—eternally. And when Jesus returns from heaven to bring about a new heaven and a new earth (see 1 Thess. 4:13–18; Rev. 21:1), he will return with a fully human nature—body and soul.

A Transformation of Humanity

Jesus, the God-man, has also restored humanity by transforming it. This transformation, however, is not through genetic engineering or artificial intelligence, as Harari suggests; it is through a resurrection.[6] In 1 Corinthians 15, the apostle Paul explains how Christ's bodily resurrection is organically linked to the future bodily resurrection of all believers. He calls it the "firstfruits of those who have fallen asleep" (15:20). Jesus's resurrection was distinct in time but inseparable in nature to what believers will one day experience. Paul continues,

> For the trumpet will sound, the dead will be raised imperishable, and we will be changed. For the perishable must clothe itself with the imperishable, and the mortal with immortality. (vv. 52–53)

When Jesus returns, believers will receive resurrection bodies just like his. They will no longer be weak, perishable, and subject to pain, suffering, or death.

And they will no longer be capable of sinning.

A little earlier in the chapter, Paul writes something that is easy to overlook but is transformative if we pause to reflect on what it teaches:

---

[6]. To explore this further, see John C. Lennox, *2084: Artificial Intelligence and the Future of Humanity* (Grand Rapids: Zondervan, 2020).

So it is written: "The first man Adam became a living being" [quoting Gen. 2:7]; the last Adam, a life-giving spirit. . . . As was the earthly man, so are those who are of the earth; and as is the heavenly man, so also are those who are of heaven. And just as we have borne the image of the earthly man, so shall we bear the image of the heavenly man. (1 Cor. 15:45–49)

What do you think Paul is contrasting here? At first glance, it is easy to assume that he is contrasting fallen Adam with the resurrected Jesus. That is unsurprising—sin contrasted with righteousness. But notice what Paul quotes in verse 45: Genesis 2:7. He is contrasting pre-fall *sinless* Adam with the resurrected Jesus.

Transformed humanity is even better than pre-fall humanity. You see, pre-fall humanity was capable of sinning—of eroding the distinction between God and humanity. But the resurrected Jesus is not. He can never sin, which means that the transformed humanity can never fall. It will forever experience the unparalleled joy of an eternally distinct yet inseparable relationship with the triune God.

Living It Out: Look Forward . . .

Too often, the good news of the gospel is presented in limp and anemic terms. Salvation is described as a "get out of jail free" card, and heaven is pictured as "pie in the sky when you die." This butchers the truth.

The Christian hope is one of re-creation into the distinct but inseparable worshipers we were created to be. When Jesus returns, we will be more human than we have ever been. We will delight to bring order and flourishing to the new creation and will experience a depth of relationship with one another and with God that we can barely begin to imagine now. All the pity parties of this life will be transformed into one gigantic praise party that will last forever. This is what we look forward to if we have repented and placed our trust in Jesus.

It has been said that the Christian life should be lived backward. We should live now in light of what we will one day be in the future. It is easy to get so fixated on our current struggle with sin that we just give up the fight.

We need to be reminded that the fight has been won by Christ on the cross and will be won in our own experience when Christ returns. These truths will give us the hope to press on now in our weakness, sadness, loneliness, and suffering.

Toward the end of Hebrews, the author exhorts his readers to persevere and points them to the example of Jesus:

> Let us run with perseverance the race marked out for us, fixing our eyes on Jesus, the pioneer and perfecter of faith. For the joy set before him he endured the cross, scorning its shame, and sat down at the right hand of the throne of God. (Heb. 12:1–2)

It was for the joy set before him that Jesus endured the cross. What was that joy? Surely it was the joy of carrying redeemed humanity into heaven, of undoing the terrible separation wrought by sin, of experiencing unencumbered love and delight with the Father and the Spirit again. That is a joy he promises to share with us. Let us fix our eyes on it. *That* is where we will find the strength, power, and desire to press on in fighting sin and living for Christ.

Making It Personal

1. What in this chapter has deepened your understanding of the gospel?
2. List five practical implications of the promised transformation of humanity. What does this hope mean for your current thoughts, actions, and attitudes?
3. How might these practical implications change the way you speak with other Christians and non-Christians in your life?
4. Spend a few minutes thanking God for the gospel truths discussed in part 2. Write down or draw some of those truths and put them somewhere prominent to help you remember the gospel and thank God.

Further Reading for Part 2

Charnock, Stephen. *Discourses on Christ Crucified*. Philadelphia: Presbyterian Board of Publication, 1841.

Gaffin, Richard B., Jr. *Resurrection and Redemption: A Study in Paul's Soteriology*. Phillipsburg, NJ: P&R Publishing, 2012.

Letham, Robert. *The Work of Christ*. Contours of Christian Theology. Leicester: IVP Academic, 1993.

Macleod, Donald. *The Person of Christ*. Contours of Christian Theology. Leicester: IVP Academic, 1998.

Murray, John. *Redemption Accomplished and Applied*. Grand Rapids: Eerdmans, 2015.

Part 3

What Is Happening in the World?

Where was God when two planes hit the Twin Towers on September 11, 2001? If God is all powerful, why doesn't he bring my best friend to faith even though I've been praying for him for the past ten years? Come to think of it, what's the point of prayer anyway? If God already knows "the end from the beginning" (Isa. 46:10), then my prayer isn't going to change anything. Nor is my evangelism, for that matter. God can bring people to faith with or without me. I might as well just live a quiet life, keep my head down, and enjoy the good things this world has to offer.

These types of questions and attitudes concern the relationship between God's sovereignty and human responsibility. They are about what is happening in the world and about God's involvement in it. Most, if not all, thinking people reflect on these matters from time to time, particularly at times of intense suffering and grief.

Indeed, for some, the very existence of suffering is a reason to reject the existence of God. The playwright George Bernard Shaw famously wrote, "How are atheists produced? Nine times out of ten something like this happens. A beloved wife or husband or child or sweetheart is gnawed to death by cancer, struck dumb by apoplexy or strangled by diphtheria. And the looker-on after praying vainly to God to refrain from such wanton and hideous cruelty indignantly repudiates his faith in the divine monster and he becomes not merely indifferent and sceptical but fiercely and actively hostile to religion."[1]

1. Quoted in H. J. Richards, *Philosophy of Religion*, 2nd ed., Heinemann Advanced Religious Studies (Oxford: Heinemann, 2000), 51.

I cannot thoroughly address all the questions relating to God's sovereignty in just a few chapters. My aim is more modest. I would like to trace out a framework for exploring the Bible's teaching on these matters in chapters 7 and 8 and then briefly apply it to them in chapter 9. Once again, the phrase "distinct but inseparable" will be key. You might think that is rather convenient, but, as we shall see, the connection flows from the fact that God's interactions with the world reflect who he is in himself.

7

GOD'S SOVEREIGNTY AND HUMAN RESPONSIBILITY

> *The Bible teaches* both *that God is sovereign* and *that humans are responsible for their voluntary actions.*

Before we dive into what the Bible teaches about God's relationship with the world, it is helpful to examine how popular alternative worldviews tackle the question.

Determinism versus Indeterminism

Let us consider two extremes.[1] One of them is determinism. In its hardest form, determinism holds that everything in the universe is determined by external forces. What humans do has no meaningful impact because, at the end of the day, the gods will decide.

Greek mythology personified this fatalistic determinism in the *Moirai*, or Fates, who spun, measured, and cut the thread of life. Fatalism is alive and well today among those who rush to read their horoscope every morning to find out what the day has in store for them. Hinduism has a myth that on

---

1. See John Frame, "Determinism, Chance and Freedom," in *New Dictionary of Christian Apologetics*, ed. W. C. Campbell-Jack and Gavin McGrath (Leicester: IVP, 2006).

the sixth day of a child's life, Brahma (god) visits the child and writes their destiny on their forehead. Fatalistic determinism even surfaces among some Muslims, who speak about the *qadar* (fate) of Allah. By this, they simply mean, "It's out of my hands. Allah decides."

Human actions are predetermined

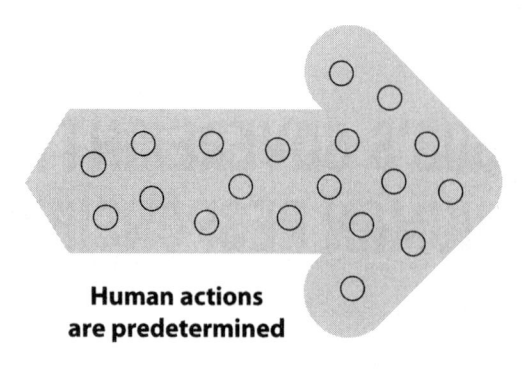

Fig. 7.1. Determinism

The other extreme is indeterminism—the view that there is no god and that external powers, natural or supernatural, do not have any bearing on our actions. Human beings are autonomous (that means "self-ruling" or "self-determining") and can do whatever they like without limitation or restraint.

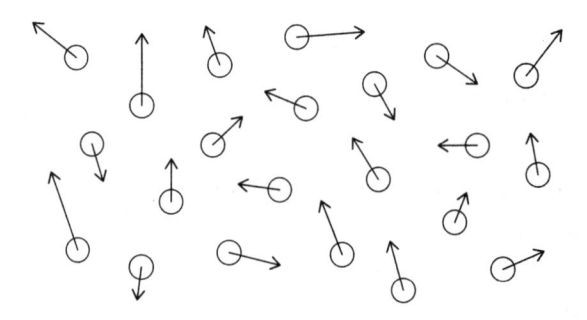

Human actions are totally free

Fig. 7.2. Indeterminism

Most people's worldview falls somewhere in between these two extremes. Some claim not to believe in God, but they still believe that some mystical force (influenced by Eastern mysticism or Star Wars) influences their actions. Others claim to believe in a God who is active in the world but say that God helps only those who help themselves. Still others profess to believe in a God who answers prayer, but they don't dare to pray anything apart from "God's will be done."

It is tempting to think that all worldviews exist somewhere on the spectrum between determinism and indeterminism—either God determines the future, and what we do doesn't matter very much, or we determine the future, and God has no say in it. When we turn to the Bible, however, we discover that it teaches two truths simultaneously: God is absolutely sovereign over the universe, and human beings are fully responsible for their actions.

God's Sovereignty

God's sovereignty is revealed throughout the Scriptures. As we saw in chapter 4, God is both the Creator and Sustainer of the universe and, as such, rules over the world that he has created. He "has established his throne in heaven, and his kingdom rules over all" (Ps. 103:19). He "works out everything in conformity with the purpose of his will" (Eph. 1:11). When earthly kings rise and fall, it is because God has ordained it. The Lord anoints David to be king over Israel (see 1 Sam. 16:1–13), and he deposes King Saul (see 1 Sam. 15:26). He even raises up the regional superpowers of Assyria and Babylon to judge his own people (see Isa. 10:5–6; Hab. 1:6). This all happens at his command and according to his plan (see Isa. 45:1). King David exclaims, "Yours, LORD, is the greatness and the power and the glory and the majesty and the splendor, for everything in heaven and earth is yours. Yours, LORD, is the kingdom; you are exalted as head over all" (1 Chron. 29:11).

We should not think, however, that God is concerned only about large civil affairs. He is intimately involved with every detail of the natural world. Jesus taught that the Father feeds the birds of the air and clothes the flowers of the field (see Matt. 6:25–34). He numbers the hairs of our heads, and not a single sparrow can drop to the ground without the Father's say-so (see Matt. 10:29–30). Indeed, God is sovereign over the very forces of nature themselves:

"Do any of the worthless idols of the nations bring rain? Do the skies themselves send down showers? No, it is you, LORD our God" (Jer. 14:22).

If God is sovereign over nature, then he is surely sovereign over our daily lives as well. Solomon writes, "Many are the plans in a person's heart, but it is the LORD's purpose that prevails" (Prov. 19:21). In a similar vein, James warns his readers against making extensive plans about the future. Instead, they should humbly say, "If it is the Lord's will, we will live and do this or that" (James 4:15). The Lord is sovereign over life and death itself: "See now that I myself am he! There is no god besides me. I put to death and I bring to life, I have wounded and I will heal, and no one can deliver out of my hand" (Deut. 32:39).

The Bible even teaches that God is sovereign over the sinful actions of humans. Pharaoh sinned by hardening his heart against the God of Israel, and yet we're also told that the *Lord* hardened Pharaoh's heart (see Ex. 11:10). Elsewhere the apostle Paul teaches that God "hardens whom he wants to harden" (Rom. 9:18). Eli's sons were "scoundrels" who "had no regard for the LORD" (1 Sam. 2:12), yet God maintained his sovereign rule over their rebellion, since it was his "will to put them to death" (1 Sam. 2:25). David's decree to take a census was a sinful act of rebellion—only the Lord had the right to number his people—and yet we're told that God incited David to number them (see 2 Sam. 24:1). God is sovereign over all the affairs of the world, and humans remain responsible for their actions.

Human Responsibility

We see human responsibility from the earliest chapters of Genesis. Adam and Eve were responsible for their decision to eat from the Tree of the Knowledge of Good and Evil, and they were judged for it (see Gen. 3:16–19). As the people of Israel stand on the edge of the promised land, about to enter, they are warned of the blessings for obedience and the curses for disobedience of God's law (see Deut. 28). Moses exhorts them, "Choose life, so that you and your children may live and that you may love the LORD your God, listen to his voice, and hold fast to him" (30:19–20).

The Scriptures are clear that humans are personally responsible for their actions (see Deut. 24:16). The Lord declares that "the one who sins is the one who will die" (Ezek. 18:20), but if a wicked person turns from their sin, they will surely live, "for [God] take[s] no pleasure in the death of anyone" (Ezek. 18:32). This emphasis on personal responsibility continues into the New Testament, where we read that people are destined to "die once, and after that to face judgment" (Heb. 9:27). God does not show favoritism—he "will repay each person according to what they have done" (Rom. 2:6; see also v. 11).

Human beings are morally responsible and will be held accountable for their thoughts, words, and actions. We will also be held accountable for the way we respond to Jesus. The people of Capernaum who refused to repent at the teaching and the miracles of Jesus were told that it will be more bearable on the day of judgment for Sodom than for them (see Matt. 11:24). Jesus called on people to "repent and believe the good news" (Mark 1:15), and this call is repeated throughout the New Testament (see Acts 2:38; 16:31; Rom. 10:9, 11).

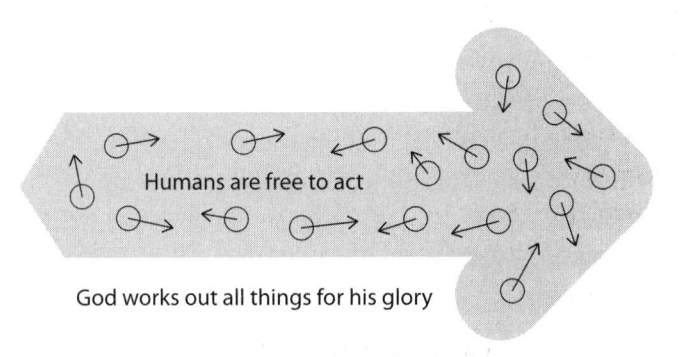

Fig. 7.3. God's Sovereignty and Human Responsibility

Free Will

You will notice that I have refrained until now from using the term *free will*. This is deliberate—not because I don't believe in the existence of free will, rightly understood, but because the concept is so easily misunderstood. When people speak about free will, they usually mean libertarian free will: the ability to make choices that are not influenced by past events, prior prejudice, current disposition, or constraints. It is the power of contrary choice, and it relies on the belief that we can make decisions from a position of pure, dispassionate neutrality.[2]

There are moral, logical, and biblical problems with this definition of free will. Morally, if we make choices from an entirely neutral standpoint, without any reason for making those choices, then it is impossible to say that they are morally significant. Our choices are simply random reflexes and are neither good nor bad.

Logically, if there is no reason for the choices we make, then they cannot be called *choices* in any meaningful sense. R.C. Sproul compares this to the situation faced by Alice in Lewis Carroll's novel *Alice's Adventures in Wonderland*: "One day Alice came to a fork in the road and saw a Cheshire cat in a tree. 'Which road do I take?' she asked. 'Where do you want to go?' was his response. 'I don't know,' Alice answered. 'Then,' said the cat, 'it doesn't matter.'"[3]

The biblical obstacles are even more considerable. The idea that humans have unbounded freedom is incompatible with God's sovereignty. Indeed, not even God has unbounded freedom. When I want to be provocative, I sometimes ask Christian friends whether there is anything that God cannot do. They sit and ponder. Instinctively, they want to say, "No, there is nothing that God cannot do. He is all-powerful!" But there are actually lots of things that God cannot do.[4] He cannot lie, he cannot change, he cannot break a promise, he cannot do evil, he cannot deny himself. God does not have the power of contrary choice in an absolute sense because he must always act consistently with his holy character; he cannot do otherwise.

Moreover, because sin has come into the world, the idea that we are somehow neutral or morally upright is utterly false. Sin has blinded our minds (see 2 Cor. 4:4; Eph. 4:17–19), and so our hearts are naturally inclined toward evil (see Gen. 6:5), with no capacity to fix themselves. We are like a shopping cart with one of its wheels out of alignment, always veering in the direction of sin.

---

2. See Scott Christensen, *What about Free Will? Reconciling Our Choices with God's Sovereignty* (Phillipsburg, NJ: P&R Publishing, 2016), 15–16.

3. Lewis Carroll, *Alice's Adventures in Wonderland*. Quoted in R.C. Sproul, *Chosen by God* (Wheaton, IL: Thomas Nelson, 1986), 52.

4. See Nick Tucker, *12 Things God Can't Do . . . and How They Can Help You to Sleep at Night* (London: The Good Book Company, 2022).

However, if we are not utterly free, how is it fair for God to hold us morally accountable for our choices? The answer, I think, is found in the fact that we act voluntarily. We do what we want to do. The eighteenth-century American theologian Jonathan Edwards described a man's freedom as "his being free from hindrance or impediment in the way of doing, or conducting in any respect, as he wills."[5] Human freedom is all about doing as we *will*—without external coercion.[6]

Living It Out: Real Responsibility

On June 7, 2020, a statue of Edward Colston, a Bristol-born merchant, philanthropist, and slave trader, was toppled from its plinth in Bristol city center, dragged through the city, and thrown into Bristol Harbor. It was one of many statues around the world that were defaced or removed following the killing of George Floyd on May 25, 2020. The toppling of the Colston statue generated much debate. Could criminal damage be justified in such circumstances?[7] Is it right to attempt to erase history when we find it embarrassing? Was Colston simply a product of his time, making it unfair to judge him by today's standards?

That last question is an interesting one. We could ask the same thing of low-ranking Nazi officers in World War II. Is it fair to judge them by today's standards? After all, those officers were raised in a culture seeped in Nazi propaganda. They didn't know any better. And their actions (like Colston's) were entirely in line with their country's law.

The understanding of human responsibility outlined above really helps us here. Both Colston and those Nazi officers probably didn't have the power of contrary choice. They certainly weren't making their decisions from a position of pure, dispassionate neutrality. And, who knows, had we been in their

---

5. Jonathan Edwards, *The Works of Jonathan Edwards*, vol. 1, *Freedom of the Will*, ed. Paul Ramsey (New Haven, CT: Yale University Press, 1957), 163.

6. The theological term for this form of responsibility is *compatibilism*. Jesus himself taught that the good person acts out of the good desires of his heart and the wicked person out of the wicked desires of his heart (see Matt 12:35). See also Frame, "Determinism, Chance and Freedom"; Christensen, *What about Free Will?*, 136–49.

7. Four people were tried for criminal damage, and all four were acquitted at their jury trial. See "Edward Colston Statue: Four Cleared of Criminal Damage," *BBC*, January 5, 2022, https://www.bbc.co.uk/news/uk-england-bristol-59727161.

position, we may well have done the same. But they *were* acting voluntarily, which means that they were morally responsible for their actions.

English criminal law distinguishes between what are called *legal defenses* and *mitigations*. If someone carjacks you, holds a gun to your head, and says, "Floor it," you will be able to plead the defense of duress when the speeding ticket comes through your door and will be found not guilty. We are only morally accountable for the things we do voluntarily—for the things we do according to our will. If, however, you were taught to drive by a father who used to race cars (as I was), and that has influenced your driving ever since, that could only be taken into account in sentencing as a mitigating factor. It would not be an excuse for the offence because you were acting voluntarily.

Let us apply this to social and ethnic tensions within the church. If you have grown up in a church that has always used the King James Version of the Bible, you may struggle when you move to a new church and find people reading from the NIV. You may even make snarky comments about it. Your upbringing and background explain why you adopt that posture, but it does not excuse any sin. You are responsible for your thoughts and actions.

Similarly, if you have grown up in an all-White, all-Black, or all-Hispanic church, you may struggle to love and accept Christians of other ethnicities and backgrounds. Indeed, the structures within those churches may make it incredibly difficult, both culturally and emotionally, for you to welcome others. In some ways, you are a victim of your circumstances and the institutional blind spots that have shaped your Christian formation. But you are still responsible for how you voluntarily respond to them. We will make progress in pursuing unity in diversity only when we step up, search our hearts, and take responsibility for our voluntary actions and choices.

Making It Personal

1. Where does your thinking tend to fall on the spectrum between determinism (everything is predetermined, humans are bound to their fate) and indeterminism (there is no ultimate purpose or direction, humans are totally free)? Why do you think that is?
2. How could thinking in terms of either extreme hinder your growth as a Christian?

3. How does the biblical view of this complex concept better fit our experience?
4. If you are discussing this book in a group, ask other members of the group how this chapter will help them next time somebody asks, "But don't we have free will?"
5. How have you been shaped by institutional and cultural blind spots? What would it look like for you to take greater responsibility for your actions and choices moving forward?

8

THE DYNAMIC OF SOVEREIGNTY AND RESPONSIBILITY

> *God's sovereignty and human responsibility operate inseparably at all times, but they are distinct because God stands behind good and evil in very different ways. This enables us to respect cultural differences while maintaining absolute moral standards.*

In the previous chapter, we saw that God's sovereignty and human responsibility are clearly taught throughout the Bible. This raises the question of how they are compatible with each other in a single event.

Inseparable

A close study of the Bible reveals that God's sovereignty and human responsibility always operate inseparably. God works out his purposes *while* humans work out theirs—often to very different ends. Let's look at a couple of examples. As I describe these familiar stories, think about the players in them and the choices they are making.

The closing chapters of Genesis (37–50) tell the story of Joseph's life. Joseph is Jacob's favorite son, and Jacob showers him with gifts, including an ornate robe. Understandably, his brothers grow jealous, and Joseph doesn't help the family harmony by sharing a dream about how his brothers, mother, and father will one day bow down before him. Eventually, the brothers hatch a plot to murder him. But at the last minute, they change their plans and sell Joseph into slavery.

Joseph ends up in Egypt, working in the home of Potiphar, Pharaoh's captain of the guard. Joseph excels in this role, and Potiphar puts him in charge of the whole household, but Potiphar's wife starts lusting after Joseph. When Joseph rebuffs her advances, she falsely accuses him and has him thrown into jail.

Meanwhile, Pharaoh has had a troubling dream. He's told that Joseph can reliably interpret dreams, so he has Joseph brought to him from the dungeon. Joseph tells Pharaoh that his dream predicts a huge famine, and he suggests a strategy to prepare Egypt for it. Canaan is not so fortunate, and Joseph's brothers are forced to travel to Egypt to beg for food.

By this time, Joseph has been promoted to the office of Pharaoh's prime minister, but his brothers don't recognize him. Eventually, Joseph reveals himself, and there's a joyful reunion. Joseph's father, Jacob, is brought up from Canaan, and there's a happy family again—or so it seems. When Jacob dies, Joseph's brothers are left with a fearful thought in the back of their minds: "Is now the time when Joseph will exact his revenge?" Joseph responds to his brothers' fears with the words "Don't be afraid. Am I in the place of God? You intended to harm me, but God intended it for good to accomplish what is now being done, the saving of many lives" (Gen. 50:19–20).

It is really important to understand what is and is not being said here about the causal factors that led to Joseph being sold into slavery and eventually elevated to the rank of prime minister. Joseph does not say that his brothers had evil plans to kill him but that somehow God managed to "pull a rabbit out of the hat" and turn it around for good. Likewise, he does not say that God originally planned to drive Joseph down to Egypt in a royal chariot but that the brothers somehow managed to scupper this plan and sell him into slavery.[1]

---

1. D. A. Carson, *How Long, O Lord? Reflections on Suffering and Evil* (Leicester: IVP, 1990), 205–6.

The Dynamic of Sovereignty and Responsibility

Joseph says that there were parallel intentions as he was sold into slavery.[2] God intended to use Joseph to save his people, while Joseph's brothers wickedly intended to be rid of their brother. God did not have to adapt his plans to fit around the actions of Joseph's brothers like a divine chess master. Nor was God somehow responsible for or implicated in the brothers' sin. God sovereignly worked out his purposes while Joseph's brothers voluntarily worked out theirs. God's sovereignty and human responsibility were inseparable.

We see exactly the same thing happening in the greatest event in human history—the death and resurrection of Jesus. Who killed Jesus? There are lots of possible answers: the Jews, the Romans, Judas. But it is also true to say that God killed Jesus—it was the triune God's eternal plan (see Gal. 4:4; Eph. 3:11; 1 Peter 1:19–21). It is even true to say that Jesus willingly went to the cross. He said, "No one takes [my life] from me, but I lay it down of my own accord. I have authority to lay it down and authority to take it up again" (John 10:18).

In his Pentecost sermon, Peter is crystal clear that the cross was, at one and the same time, God's sovereign plan and the act of wicked and accountable human beings: "This man was handed over to you by God's deliberate plan and foreknowledge; and you, with the help of wicked men, put him to death by nailing him to the cross" (Acts 2:23).

The same point is made two chapters later when Peter and John are released from prison and join the Jerusalem church in prayer (see Acts 4:24). They begin by praising the "Sovereign Lord," celebrating his creation of the heavens and the earth. They quote from Psalm 2:1–2, which confirms the historic pattern of humans plotting against the Lord, and then they continue:

> Indeed Herod and Pontius Pilate met together with the Gentiles and the people of Israel in this city to conspire against your holy servant Jesus, whom you anointed. They did what your power and will had decided beforehand should happen. (Acts 27–28)

---

2. John Frame writes the following: "Again and again, it is God who brings about each event, good or evil, for his good purposes. God did not merely allow Joseph to be sent into Egypt; rather, God himself sends him, though certainly the treacherous brothers are responsible. Throughout the Scriptures, God stands behind each great historical event." John Frame, *Systematic Theology: An Introduction to Christian Belief* (Phillipsburg, NJ: P&R Publishing, 2013), 149. See also Scott Christensen, *What about Free Will? Reconciling Our Choices with God's Sovereignty* (Phillipsburg, NJ: P&R Publishing, 2016), 45–46.

Notice carefully what Peter and John are saying here. Herod, Pontius Pilate, the Gentiles, and the Jews are all morally responsible for their actions. The cross was the ultimate act of culpable rebellion, as humanity united to murder God's anointed King. And yet the prayer also attributes these events to God's good will. The word used here is *proorizō*, which means "predetermined." In eternity past, God determined what would happen.

Once again, the parallel intentions are inseparable, but God is neither constrained by human actions nor implicated in their guilt. This is because God's sovereignty and human responsibility are not only inseparable—they are also distinct.

Distinct

What does it mean to say that God's sovereignty and human responsibility are distinct? It means that God stands behind good and evil in different ways. Theologian Don Carson describes this well: "God stands behind evil in such a way that not even evil takes place outside the bounds of his sovereignty, yet the evil is not morally chargeable to him: it is always chargeable to secondary agents, to secondary causes. On the other hand, God stands behind good in such a way that it not only takes place within the bounds of his sovereignty, but it is always chargeable to him, and only derivatively to secondary agents."[3]

Carson introduces the language of primary and secondary agents here. That may sound confusing, but we are actually quite familiar with these concepts. My two boys love playing soccer, and my eldest, Zach, loves scoring goals. Now, when Zach scores a goal, who caused that goal? I taught Zach how to score in the top corner (he calls it "top bins"); in fact, I taught him how to kick a ball, and, for that matter, I taught him how to walk. In a sense, I was the primary agent of his goal, and he was the secondary agent—but my contribution to the goal was so remote that I deserve no credit for it.

When my eldest, Sophie, started school at age four, I was shocked by the swear words her classmates were using. Sophie didn't even know what the words meant. The reason, of course, was that those were the words her classmates were hearing at home. The parents were the primary agents in

---

3. Carson, *How Long, O Lord?*, 213.

The Dynamic of Sovereignty and Responsibility

the swearing, and the children were the secondary agents—but this time the contribution of the primary agents was so direct that it was morally chargeable to them.[4]

God is sovereign over everything. He stands behind both good and evil, but he does so in different ways. God is so causally remote from evil that it cannot be charged to him (see Hab. 1:13; 1 John 1:5), and he is so causally essential to all that is good in the world that every good work can and must be ultimately credited to him (see Ps. 16:2; Isa. 64:4; John 15:5). A few examples from the Bible will illustrate this dynamic.

First, it is interesting to compare the anointing of David (see 1 Sam. 16) with that of Jehu (see 2 Kings 9). Both are anointed king before they ascend to the throne, but they respond to this news in very different ways. David continues working as a shepherd, and, although he enjoys a bit of fame after his great victory over Goliath, he is subsequently mistreated, persecuted, and abused by King Saul. David knows that God has anointed him king, but he also knows that Saul remains God's anointed king until God brings about a transition of power.

On a number of occasions, David and his men have the opportunity to kill Saul and speed up the process. But David resists, telling his men, "The LORD forbid that I should do such a thing to my master, the LORD's anointed, or lay my hand on him; for he is the anointed of the LORD" (1 Sam. 24:6). Eventually, Saul takes his own life in battle, and David is crowned king.

Throughout the whole account, we see that God is sovereign but that he works out his purposes within his own time frame. He does not need David to expedite matters by murdering Saul—instead, David acts uprightly, faithfully, and patiently, showing himself to be a man after God's own heart (see 1 Sam. 13:14).

The contrast with Jehu could not be more dramatic. Elisha sends a young prophet to Ramoth Gilead to anoint Jehu king of Israel (see 2 Kings 9:1). At the time, Jehu is serving as one of King Joram's commanders. He is supposed to be one of Joram's most loyal men, but he wastes no time in killing off both Joram and his *entire* family. He even murders King

---

4. John Calvin distinguished between "remote" and "proximate" causes. See John Calvin, *Concerning the Eternal Predestination of God* (London: James Clarke and Co., 1961), 122; cited in Frame, *Systematic Theology*, 295–96.

Ahaziah of Judah, simply because Ahaziah was in Joram's presence (see 2 Kings 9:27–29). Jehu has a lust for power and bloodshed—clearly he is not a man after God's own heart. Instead, a damning judgment is passed on him at the end of his life: "Jehu was not careful to keep the law of the Lord, the God of Israel, with all his heart. He did not turn away from the sins of Jeroboam" (2 Kings 10:31).

In both accounts, we see that God is sovereign in the transition of power. In no sense is his sovereignty undermined by human sin. Yet the human actors remain responsible for their actions. Human responsibility is distinct—God is not implicated in Jehu's sin—but inseparable from God's sovereignty on both occasions.

The biblical accounts of two pagan kings help us to see how God stands behind good and evil in different ways. The first king is Abimelek, king of Gerar. Abraham enters the territory of Gerar and stays there for a while (see Gen. 20:1). He's afraid that the people will kill him in order to take his wife, Sarah, so he tells the people that Sarah is his sister. On this basis, Abimelek takes Sarah to be his wife, which prompts God to confront him in a dream.

When Abimelek pleads his innocence before God, declaring that he did not know that Sarah was Abraham's wife and that he had not touched her anyway, God's response is illuminating: "Yes, I know you did this with a clear conscience, and so I have kept you from sinning against me. That is why I did not let you touch her" (Gen. 20:6). God did not let Abimelek touch Sarah. He stood behind Abimelek's good conscience and righteous actions in such a way that he can be credited for them.

We may contrast this with the king of Babylon. In Isaiah 47:6, we are told that God, in his sovereignty, gave his people into Babylon's hand. Babylon acted as an agent of God's wrath in executing judgment on Judah. But Babylon did this in a sinful and presumptuous way—thus, God pronounces judgment on them:

> You have trusted in your wickedness
>   and have said, "No one sees me."
> Your wisdom and knowledge mislead you
>   when you say to yourself,
>   "I am, and there is none besides me."

> Disaster will come upon you,
>   and you will not know how to conjure it away.
> A calamity will fall upon you
>   that you cannot ward off with a ransom;
> a catastrophe you cannot foresee
>   will suddenly come upon you. (vv. 10–11)

Babylon acted as if it were God. It said, "I am forever—the eternal queen!" (v. 7). Therefore, even though the people of Babylon fulfilled God's purposes of judgment, they did so in a wicked and sinful way for which they alone were accountable. God cannot be blamed for their sin and presumption.

To repeat, God's sovereignty and human responsibility are distinct but inseparable. God is sovereign over everything, even over our sin, but he stands behind good and evil in different ways, such that he is ultimately responsible for all that is good but never responsible for evil.[5]

It may be difficult to wrap our heads around this distinction, but we are helped if we understand that the distinct but inseparable relationship between sovereignty and responsibility flows out of God's own nature, which is both transcendent (over and above creation) and immanent (present in his world and in his relationship with what he has created). This lays the groundwork for absolute moral standards in a world of diverse cultures and moral perspectives.

Living It Out: How to Condemn Abuse while Avoiding Cultural Imperialism

In our discussion of free will in the previous chapter, we briefly touched on the morality of the choices we make. Have you ever stopped to consider how we decide whether something is right or wrong, good or bad?

Many assume that moral judgments are just a product of our upbringing. If we grow up in the West, then we will adopt Judeo-Christian values; in China, we naturally assume Confucian or Communist ideas; if we are raised in Iran, our dominant moral matrix is Islamic. The argument goes that

---

5. See Frame, *Systematic Theology*, 282–303.

all those different moral outlooks are both personal and culturally relative. To insist on one over and against the others would be cultural imperialism. Do you agree?

In 2007, the *New York Times* published an opinion piece by University of Chicago anthropologist Richard Shweder.[6] In it, he mentions an ancient Afghan cultural practice, *Bacha bāzī*, whereby older men recruit young boys in order to have sex with them. Shweder explained how the US military had been advised against trying to stop this practice—apparently, he found this advice "heartwarming"! I'm sure I'm not alone in strongly disagreeing with Shweder. *Bacha bāzī* is child abuse and must be called out as evil, regardless of how long it has been practiced or who says we shouldn't condemn it.

Yet, how *do* we respond to the question of why our moral values should trump those of the Afghan military leaders? Ultimately, the only sound answer we can give is that there is a higher moral authority that takes precedence over all others. For that to be true, the said moral authority must be absolute. It must stand outside of space and time so that it is neither subjective nor relative. The authority must be objective, timeless, and culturally transcendent. It must be God himself.

There is a second question, however: Where do moral obligations come from? What creates laws? We sometimes speak of the "law of gravity"—if an apple becomes detached from a tree, it will fall to the ground. But that is a different sort of law. It is not a moral law but rather a law of nature—it explains how things are. It does not tell us how things ought to be. Moral laws are about "ought" rather than "is." I ought to love my children, I ought to pay my window cleaner, I ought not to speed.

Further, moral obligations are always and only ever derived from personal relationships. I do not owe an obligation to a tree. If I were to burn down an entire forest, I would not have sinned against the trees—but I may have sinned against other people. For example, if the forest belonged to my neighbor, I would have breached my moral duty to that neighbor. Even if the forest belonged to me, I may have breached a broader civic obligation

---

6. Richard A. Shweder, "A True Culture War," *New York Times*, October 27, 2007, https://www.nytimes.com/2007/10/27/opinion/27shweder.html. This article is referenced by Tim Keller in his 2015 sermon on Acts 17:16–34 at Redeemer Presbyterian Church.

to minimize carbon emissions.[7] Moral obligations are owed only within the context of a personal relationship.

Let's tie this together. If ultimate values can be found only in an absolute authority, and if moral obligations can be owed only within the context of a personal relationship, then ultimate moral obligations must be derived from an absolute, personal authority.[8] As we saw in part 1, that precisely describes the God of the Bible. He is absolute yet personal. In the language of philosophy, he is both transcendent and immanent.

It is because of God's transcendent and immanent nature that the distinct yet inseparable relationship between God's sovereignty and human responsibility is inevitable. God's sovereignty is grounded in his transcendence; our responsibility flows from God's personal relationship with us. Now, it is mysterious that God can be both transcendent and immanent, but mystery is not the same as contradiction—and, as we saw in part 1, comprehension (exhaustive knowledge) of God is beyond our grasp. This is why we affirm what we know to be true about God's relationship with the world—he is sovereign, and we are responsible—without knowing exactly how that works out.

It is also why we can trust the Bible's teaching that God stands behind good and evil in very different ways. His mysterious nature, both transcendent and immanent, enables us to speak of good and evil in absolute terms that are not culturally contingent. We can respect certain cultural practices of Afghan people while maintaining that *bacha bāzī* is evil; we can appreciate Indian food, dress, and music while condemning the (now illegal) practice of *sati*, in which widows burn themselves alive on the funeral pyres of their husbands; we can affirm the benefits of a free market while lamenting Western greed.

A God who is both transcendent and immanent necessitates the distinct but inseparable relationship between God's sovereignty and human responsibility.[9] He also enables a diverse people to respect and appreciate cultural differences while insisting on a set of absolute and timeless moral standards.

---

7. I realize that climate change is a controversial topic, but hopefully it makes my point!
8. See John Frame's excellent explanation of this in John M. Frame, *Apologetics to the Glory of God: An Introduction* (Phillipsburg, NJ: P&R Publishing, 1994), 93–102.
9. See further D. A. Carson, *Divine Sovereignty and Human Responsibility: Biblical Perspectives in Tension* (Grand Rapids: Baker, 1994), 209–12; Carson, *How Long, O Lord?*, 215–18.

Making It Personal

1. What concept(s) from this chapter do you find most difficult to understand? God's sovereignty and human responsibility? God as both immanent and transcendent? God as absolute authority?
2. How are you tempted to shirk responsibility for the wrong you do?
3. Do you ever blame God for what others have done to harm you? How could Carson's explanation of primary and secondary agents help you to address this?
4. How does God's absolute yet personal nature inform the way we should relate to him?
5. In your context, what culturally accepted sins need to be confronted by the absolute moral standards of God?
6. Ask the Spirit to enlighten your mind, that you may understand (even if you may not comprehend) these truths in a transformative way.

9

LIVING RESPONSIBLY UNDER GOD'S SOVEREIGNTY

> *Grasping that God's sovereignty and human responsibility are distinct but inseparable helps us to understand our role in evangelism and prayer and to navigate suffering and decision-making.*

In chapter 7, we examined the Bible's teaching that God is absolutely sovereign and that humans are responsible for their actions. In chapter 8, we scrutinized the dynamic between these two truths and saw that they are distinct but inseparable. God sovereignly stands behind both good and evil, but he does so in a distinct way that does not exonerate humans for their sinful actions or impute responsibility for evil to God. In this chapter, we will explore how the framework for understanding the relationship between God's sovereignty and human responsibility can be applied to four specific areas of life. As such, this whole chapter may be considered a "Living It Out" application of what we have studied in part 3.

Decision-Making

Decision-making can be hard, especially if we fear that we might step outside the bounds of God's will. What career does God want me to pursue?

Where does he want me to live? Whom does he want me to marry? Some Christians assume that God has a plan mapped out for their lives, which he has stored away in some filing cabinet in heaven, and that their job is to discover this plan and follow it. Living life this way can be exhausting, like walking on a tightrope, as we are forever nervous about falling out of God's will for our lives.

What we've seen in the past couple of chapters should be a great relief for those who are stuck on the tightrope. God is sovereign over all things. He does have a plan that he will fulfill, but he has revealed only some of that plan to us. Our responsibility, which is distinct (in that we are capable of sin) but inseparable (in that God still reigns) from God's sovereign plan, is to obey what God *has* revealed.

Theologians distinguish between God's decretal will and his moral will. God's decretal will is what God has decided *will* happen. Most of this is not revealed to us. For example, he has not told us when the sparrow that perches on the tree in our garden will drop to the ground (see Matt. 10:29). Those things that he has revealed—such as the second coming of Christ—we know very little about and have no control over. God's moral will is what *ought* to be. An example is found in 1 John 2:15–17:

> Do not love the world or anything in the world. If anyone loves the world, love for the Father is not in them. For everything in the world—the lust of the flesh, the lust of the eyes, and the pride of life—comes not from the Father but from the world. The world and its desires pass away, but whoever does the will of God lives forever.

God's moral will is that we do not live according to the desires of the flesh but instead desire what God desires—a life full of love and holiness. That is what *ought* to be, and we have a responsibility to walk in obedience to God's moral will. But because we are not robots and thus act according to our own personal wills, it is possible for us to disobey God's moral will (even as Christians), and this has been permitted within God's decretal will.

In sum, God's decretal will is what God has said *will* be. Because God is sovereign, it will always happen. God's moral will is what God has said *ought* to be, and because we are morally responsible, we may thwart it by our actions.

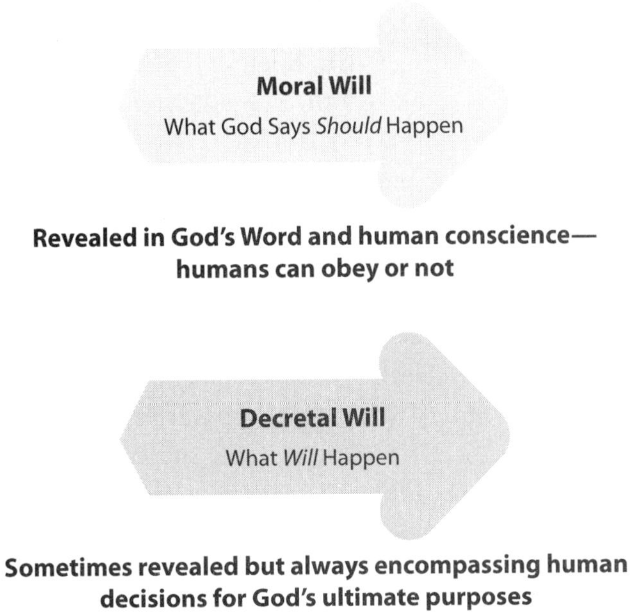

Moral Will

What God Says *Should* Happen

Revealed in God's Word and human conscience—humans can obey or not

Decretal Will

What *Will* Happen

Sometimes revealed but always encompassing human decisions for God's ultimate purposes

Fig. 9.1. God's Moral and Decretal Will

All of this is a great help in decision-making. God has not revealed his decretal will to us concerning what job we should do, where we should live, or whom we should marry. When making decisions about such things, our aim is simply to follow God's moral will.

Following God's moral will rules out some decisions: we should not work as a burglar or marry someone of the same sex. It also informs our decision-making in subtler ways. For example, the responsibility to provide for our family (see 1 Tim. 5:8) means that we ought to seek work with the hours and the salary to accomplish this. There is, however, a wide margin of freedom in how we walk wisely within God's moral will, and there are a number of good books that can help us think through it further.[1]

---

1. See, for example, Kevin DeYoung, *Just Do Something: A Liberating Approach to Finding God's Will* (Chicago: Moody Press, 2014); Phillip D. Jensen and Tony Payne, *Guidance and the Voice of God*, Guidebooks for Life (Sydney: Matthias Press, 1997); Scott Christensen, *What about Free Will? Reconciling Our Choices with God's Sovereignty* (Phillipsburg, NJ: P&R Publishing, 2016), 85–88.

Suffering

Making sense of suffering is hard whether you are an atheist or a Christian. We all face suffering in one form or another, and so it makes sense for us to prepare ourselves for those times. How does what we have seen in chapters 7 and 8 help us to prepare?

First, human responsibility explains how suffering entered the world. The universe was created by God to be full of love, joy, peace, and flourishing. Human sin disrupted that by bringing suffering and death into the world. Sometimes we suffer because of our own sins—a husband is left by his wife following his adulterous affair, for example. Sometimes we suffer at the sinful hands of others—a family is left bereaved by a driver's decision to get into her car while drunk. At other times, we suffer because God is disciplining us as children so that we can share his holiness (see Heb. 12:7–11). At still other times, as in the case of Job, we may suffer for reasons not known to us.

People do not suffer in proportion to their sin—this is the hugely damaging mistake that Job's friends made. Some evil people live relatively pain-free lives, and some very good people suffer immensely, just like Job. But Jesus *does* teach that all suffering should point us to the problem of human sin and lead us to the only One who can save us (see Luke 13:1–5).

God's sovereignty should also comfort us in the face of suffering and death. Romans 8:28 is not a passage we ought to turn to for the first time when we are in the crucible of suffering—it's a passage we should etch into our hearts and minds so that we are ready to suffer well as Christians. "In all things," suffering included, "God works for the good of those who love him, who have been called according to his purpose" (Rom. 8:28).

We distinguished God's decretal will and moral will above. This distinction helps us here as well. God has decreed that death and suffering would come into the world, but he has also decreed that they will end. In Revelation 20:14, we read that death and Hades (the holding place for the dead) will be thrown into the lake of fire, and then we are given this beautiful picture of how God will comfort us in our suffering: "'He will wipe every tear from [our] eyes. There will be no more death' or mourning or crying or pain, for the old order of things has passed away" (Rev. 21:4). This is because of God's moral will.

Sin, suffering, and death ought not to be in the world. God recoils at them. Faced with the death of his dear friend Lazarus, Jesus was "deeply moved in spirit and troubled" (John 11:33). That's toned down a bit in our modern translations. The word used for "troubled" in verse 33 is also used in Mark 14:5 to describe the disciples as they harshly rebuke a woman who poured expensive perfume on Jesus's head. Jesus is fuming at death and suffering. He hates it. The sovereign God takes "no pleasure in the death of anyone" (Ezek. 18:32). And it is this compassion for lost humanity that led him to take on human flesh and vanquish suffering and death forever.[2]

During the immense frustration and disappointment of the civil rights movement, Martin Luther King Jr.'s tenacious grip on the sovereignty of God kept him going. He realized that human sin and vested interests might prevent him from seeing victory in the struggle for equal rights within his lifetime. Nevertheless, he trusted that freedom would be won because the "sacred heritage of our nation and the eternal will of the almighty God are embodied in our echoing demands." King was convinced that "the arc of the moral universe is long, but it bends toward justice."

Modern minds may be tempted to squeeze King's words into a secular mold, but King was clear that his hope for change rested on God's sovereignty. He ended his "Remaining Awake through a Great Revolution" speech by quoting from Revelation 21:1 and looking forward to "a new day of justice and brotherhood and peace" in which "the sons of God will shout for joy."[3]

All forms of injustice (racial, socioeconomic, gender, and so on) violate God's moral will. He hates the pain and suffering that injustice causes, but our ultimate hope lies in God's revealed decretal will: his promise that one day injustice will be no more, and a great multitude from every nation, tribe, people, and tongue will join together to worship Christ (see Rev. 7:9).

Prayer

If God is sovereign over everything, what is the point of prayer? The answer is that God sovereignly works to fulfill his purposes in response to the prayers of his people. Two examples will help to illustrate this.

---

2. For a fuller treatment of God's sovereignty and suffering, see D. A. Carson, *How Long, O Lord? Reflections on Suffering and Evil* (Leicester: IVP, 1990).

3. Martin Luther King Jr., "Remaining Awake through a Great Revolution" (speech, National Cathedral, Washington, D.C., March 31, 1968).

First, in Exodus 32, Moses comes down from Mount Sinai after receiving the law and discovers that the Israelites have been using their spare time to craft a golden calf to worship. God is righteously angry and tells Moses that he is about to destroy the Israelites (see v. 10). Moses pleads with the Lord to relent, giving two reasons: (1) so that God's name may be glorified rather than maligned by the Egyptians (see v. 12), and (2) so that God's promise to provide numerous descendants to Abraham might still be fulfilled (see v. 13).

We then read something astonishing: "Then the LORD relented and did not bring on his people the disaster he had threatened" (v. 14). The word "relent" literally means repent: this is an example of anthropomorphism (attributing human characteristics to non-human entities—in this case, to God), and it communicates that God changed his mind regarding his people as a result of Moses's prayer.[4]

Now, we must be clear that Moses did not twist God's arm here, convincing him to do something that he did not otherwise want to do. Rather, having heard God's word of judgment, Moses speaks God's word of promise back to him in a plea for mercy. Ultimately, we see how God can simultaneously punish sin and fulfill his promise to Abraham only when a prophet greater than Moses (see Deut. 18:15) comes to represent his people on the cross. It was there that God was supremely glorified as he executed justice and poured out mercy on his people.

The second example is found in Daniel 9. As Daniel worked in Babylon, he remembered that God had promised through the prophet Jeremiah that the exile would last only seventy years (see Dan. 9:2). That time was nearly up. Now, what would you do if you were in Daniel's shoes? Throw a party and crack open a bottle of Babylon's finest Bollinger champagne, perhaps? Daniel prays. He confesses his own sins as well as those of the people. He praises God's character, pleads for his mercy, and asks God to glorify himself: "Lord, listen! Lord, forgive! Lord, hear and act! For your sake, my God, do not delay, because your city and your people bear your Name" (v. 19).

---

4. God, of course, remains unchanging (immutable). See John Frame, *Systematic Theology: An Introduction to Christian Belief* (Phillipsburg, NJ: P&R Publishing, 2013), 368–77.

After Daniel prays, the angel Gabriel visits him and tells him that his prayer was answered as soon as he began to pray (see v. 23). God acts through the prayers of his people to achieve his sovereign purposes.

The nineteenth-century preacher Charles Spurgeon said that prayer is like a homing pigeon.[5] It begins in the heart of God, God sends it to the heart of his people, and then his people send it back to his heart. That is exactly right. Prayer begins with God as he reveals his purposes in his Word. His people receive the Word in their hearts and then pray it back to him. Finally, God works.

Prayer is God's appointed means for fulfilling his sovereign purposes. This has startling implications for prayerless believers. Don Carson put it well: "If I do not pray, it is not as if the God-appointed end fails, leaving God somewhat frustrated. Instead . . . my prayerlessness, for which I am entirely responsible, cannot itself escape the reaches of God's sovereignty, forcing me to conclude that in that case there are other God-appointed ends in view, possibly including judgment on me and on those for whom I should have been interceding!"[6]

This is a sobering statement. God is sovereign, and he will work out his purposes—but we are responsible to pray. Those two things are distinct but inseparable, which means that my failure to pray may indicate that God's plan for me and for those around me entails judgment rather than blessing. May this spur all of us to pray.

Evangelism

There is a school of theological thought known as hyper-Calvinism. It has nothing to do with the Reformer John Calvin (who would have been pretty shocked by it, I suspect). Hyper-Calvinists believe that, because only those whom God has chosen (the elect) can be saved, and because we do not know who the elect are, we should not go out and offer the gospel to everyone.

You can see how that would stifle evangelism, can't you! Hyper-Calvinists are not worried about that, though, because they believe that God will simply

---

5. See C. H. Spurgeon, "Hindrances to Prayer," (speech, September 13, 1874), https://ccel.org/ccel/spurgeon/sermons20/sermons20.xliii.html.

6. D. A. Carson, *A Call to Spiritual Reformation: Priorities from Paul and His Prayers* (Leicester: IVP, 1992), 165.

bring the elect to them. You can see the logic that led them to this position, but they fail to maintain the biblical distinction between God's sovereignty in election and the Christian's responsibility to preach the gospel indiscriminately (Mark 4:1–20).

It is striking that one of the lengthiest expositions of God's sovereignty (Rom. 9:1–29) is followed immediately by one of the clearest statements on the need for evangelism and for a personal response to the gospel (Rom. 10:1–15). Paul insists that any who declare with their mouth, "Jesus is Lord" (repentance) and believe in their heart that God raised him from the dead (faith) will be saved (Rom. 10:9). People can respond this way, however, only if the gospel is first preached to them: "How can they believe in the one of whom they have not heard? And how can they hear without someone preaching to them?" (Rom. 10:14).

Throughout the New Testament, God's sovereignty in election and the church's responsibility in evangelism are taught side by side. They are distinct but inseparable. The preaching of the gospel is the means by which God brings people to salvation, and God's sovereignty gives us confidence that he can save even the most unlikely people. As the apostle Paul put it in 2 Corinthians 4:2, 6, we "[set] forth the truth plainly" (our responsibility), knowing that God "made his light shine in our hearts" (God's sovereignty).[7]

God's sovereignty and human responsibility are distinct but inseparable in evangelism. This should give us great boldness, confidence, and expectation as we share the gospel because we know that we are carrying out God's sovereign plan and trusting him with the results.

Making It Personal

1. Do you ever feel like you're "walking on a tightrope . . . forever nervous about falling out of God's will"?
2. What concepts in this chapter demonstrate that you don't have to feel this way as a Christian?

---

[7]. For a fuller discussion of God's sovereignty and evangelism, see J. I. Packer, *Evangelism and the Sovereignty of God* (Downers Grove, IL: IVP, 1961).

3. How could differentiating between God's decretal will and his moral will help you make decisions?
4. How does the knowledge that God's sovereignty and human responsibility are distinct but inseparable inform our suffering? Our prayers? Our evangelism?
5. Take a moment to ask the Spirit to enlighten your mind so that you may understand these truths in a transformative way.
6. What questions remain unanswered? Consult the recommended further reading to delve deeper into these topics.

Further Reading for Part 3

Carson, D. A. *A Call to Spiritual Reformation: Priorities from Paul and His Prayers*. Leicester: IVP, 1992.

———. *How Long, O Lord? Reflections on Suffering and Evil*. Leicester: IVP, 1990.

Christensen, Scott. *What about Free Will? Reconciling Our Choices with God's Sovereignty*. Phillipsburg, NJ: P&R Publishing, 2016.

Frame, John. Chapters 8, 9, 12, and 15 of *Systematic Theology: An Introduction to Christian Belief*. Phillipsburg, NJ: P&R Publishing, 2013.

Packer, J. I. *Evangelism and the Sovereignty of God*. Downers Grove, IL: IVP, 1961.

Part 4

What Is a Christian?

Picture the scene. It's the day of judgment. The books have been opened, and everyone is standing before the throne of God's justice.

One man confidently steps forward. He's wearing his Sabbath best and has a leather-bound copy of the Torah tucked under his arm. He begins to make his case before God: "I kept every one of the Old Testament laws without exception, I memorized the Psalms and sung them every night before going to bed, I've given regularly to the poor, and I always keep the Sabbath. And not once—not once—has a piece of crispy bacon passed my lips!"

The man looks ever so proud of himself. But then Jesus turns to him and utters these crushing words: "I never knew you. Away from me, you evildoer!" (see Matt. 7:23).

Another man steps forward. He looks uncertain, as if he doesn't quite know what he's doing there.

The court clerk asks, "Name?"

"Oh, Benjamin, sir."

"Occupation?"

The man shifts uneasily. With an apologetic tone, he replies, "Well, I guess you could say I was a professional robber!"

There's silence around the room. The clerk continues, "What good things have you done in your life, Benjamin?"

"Not much, I guess," he replies. "I helped an old lady across the road once, but, to be honest, I've been pretty nasty most of my life."

"So, what brings you here, Benjamin?" the clerk asks.

Benjamin slowly raises his stubby finger and points to Jesus, who sits high up on the judgment seat: "That man up there. He was hanging on the cross right next to me! And he said, 'Come.' So I came."

At that, Jesus opens his arms to Benjamin and, through tears, says, "Welcome, Benjamin. I'm so glad you're here. Come share my joy and meet our heavenly Father!" (see Luke 23:39–43).

That is the gospel of grace—the good news we looked at in part 2. It's news about what God has done for us, not advice about what we must do for him. And it is news of a free gift to be received by faith. We contribute nothing to our salvation except the sin from which we need to be saved. Our good works play no part. We know that, don't we? It is the heart of the Christian faith.

And yet, there's more to be said, isn't there? We know that the thief on the cross, who entered paradise on the very day he professed faith, was the exception rather than the norm. We know that the same Bible that teaches salvation by grace—"For it is by grace you have been saved, through faith —and this is not from yourselves, it is the gift of God" (Eph. 2:8)—also declares with equal clarity that "without holiness no one will see the Lord" (Heb. 12:14).

When I first heard the gospel of grace, one of the first questions I asked was "Well, does that mean that I get to live however I like?" I was relieved to discover that the apostle Paul asked this very same question (albeit rhetorically) two thousand years earlier and that he gave an unequivocal answer: "By no means!" (Rom. 6:2).

So how do we reconcile the gospel of grace with the radical calls to holiness that we find in the Bible? The answer is to be found in rightly understanding our identity in Christ and in seeing how the benefits of our union with Christ are to be received distinctly yet inseparably from one another through this union.

10

CHRISTIAN IDENTITY

> *The great news of the gospel is that God has given us himself. Christian identity is fundamentally found in our union with God in Christ. Everything else flows from that.*

The label *Christian* is used only three times in the Bible: Acts 11:26, Acts 26:28, and 1 Peter 4:16. It's not a bad label for believers, but a far more common way of describing disciples in the New Testament is to say that they are "in Christ."

Union with Christ

The apostle Paul starts most of his letters by describing his readers as those who are "in Christ," and he goes on to use the phrase "in Christ" more than eighty times in his writings. He uses a host of metaphors to illustrate the concept—a body (see 1 Cor. 12:12–26), clothing (see Eph. 4:20–28), a marriage (Eph. 5:22–33)—and declares that he considers all of his works "garbage," that he "may gain Christ and be found *in him*" (Phil. 3:8, 9).

Similarly, Peter celebrates that his readers are "in Christ" (1 Peter 5:14) and describes how they have been enabled to "participate in the divine nature" through Christ (2 Peter 1:4).

Jesus himself told his disciples that they would soon know that "I am in my Father, and you are in me, and I am in you" (John 14:20). He then illustrated this using the image of a vine: "I am the vine; you are the branches. If you remain in me and I in you, you will bear much fruit; apart from me you can do nothing" (John 15:5). Jesus wants his disciples to understand that following him means being united to him in a real, organic, life-giving, and transformative way.

This is the heart of a Christian's identity. We are one with Christ, united to him through faith. The great Reformer John Calvin wrote of this union, "That joining together of Head and members, that indwelling of Christ in our hearts—in short, that mystical union—are accorded by us the highest degree of importance, so that Christ, having been made ours, makes us sharers with him in the gifts with which he has been endowed."[1]

As we saw in chapter 5, the good news of the Christian faith is Jesus's work in time and history. The good news for us is that we get Christ! Through faith, we are united to him by a spiritual bond. The great separation between God and humanity has been dissolved. Now we can be united to God again in Christ, and this new identity will shape our being, thinking, flourishing, and interacting with the world around us. That is the grace of the gospel.

What Is Grace?

Much of what I have written so far in this book would be enthusiastically affirmed by a Roman Catholic. They would say a hearty "amen" to part 1 on the Trinity and would largely agree with what I have written on the incarnation and God's sovereignty in parts 2 and 3, but we have reached a point at which our paths diverge—the topic of grace.

Let me briefly outline the Roman Catholic understanding of grace. The Catechism of the Catholic Church describes grace as "favour, the free and undeserved help that God gives us to respond to his call to become children of God."[2] Grace is conveyed, according to the Catholic Church, through the means of grace, which are the seven sacraments (baptism, the Eucharist, confirmation, penance, anointing the sick, marriage, and holy orders), prayer,

---

1. John Calvin, *Institutes of the Christian Religion*, ed. John T. McNeill, trans. Ford Lewis Battles (Philadelphia: Westminster John Knox Press, 1960), 3.11.10.
2. United States Conference of Catholic Bishops, *Catechism of the Catholic Church*, 2nd ed. (Vatican City: Libreria Editrice Vaticana, 2012), 3.1.3.2.2.

and good works.[3] Understood in this way, grace is a thing or a substance that God infuses into or transfers to us.

An illustration might help here. Imagine that every human being is a jug. The Roman Catholic teaching is that, at the point of birth, we are all empty, but we can be filled with grace as babies through the sacrament of baptism. They understand this to be the first justification—the first declaration of our right standing before God.[4]

Over time, this grace is diminished through our sin. Fortunately, it is possible to top off the grace through the sacraments of penance and the Eucharist and through doing good works. That fills the jug again. At the end of our lives, we will be judged (the second justification) on the evidence of grace in our lives—how full our jug is. This will lead to differing degrees of justification, depending on the grace we've received and what we've done with it.[5]

This view was vigorously opposed in the sixteenth century by a movement across Europe that came to be known as the Protestant Reformation. Leading figures such as Martin Luther, Huldrych Zwingli, and John Calvin called the church to return to Scripture as its supreme authority. This resulted in much social and political upheaval, but the primary cry of the Reformers was that salvation, according to the Bible, is by grace alone (*sola gratia*), through faith alone (*sola fide*), in Christ alone (*solus Christus*).

The Protestant Reformers rejected the Roman Catholic Church's claim that we contribute in any way to our salvation by our good works. Salvation is by faith alone. And they insisted that grace is not a thing, like a liquid, but rather a person—the Lord Jesus Christ. Salvation is to be found in Christ alone because he is grace from God. As Paul wrote, "the grace of God has appeared that offers salvation to all people" (Titus 2:11). God's gift to a perishing world was not a substance conveyed by the sacraments—it was his own Son (see John 3:16).

---

3. In part 5, we will consider the Reformed understanding of the means of grace and how this differs from the teaching of the Roman Catholic Church.
4. Ludwig Ott, *Fundamentals of Catholic Dogma*, ed. James Canon Bastible, trans. Patrick Lynch (1952; repr., St. Louis: B. Herder, 1955), 251. Cited in Wayne Grudem, *Systematic Theology: An Introduction to Biblical Doctrine* (Leicester: IVP, 1994), 728.
5. Council of Trent, Session 6.7.

A Tragic Separation

Imagine being a fly on the wall at Buckingham Palace. It's the king's birthday, and he's invited his eldest son, William, for afternoon tea. They settle down on the grand sofas in the White Drawing Room and sip on their Earl Greys. William turns to King Charles and says in a quiet voice, "I love having you as my daddy!"

The king is a little taken aback by this sudden show of affection, so he replies, "Oh William, that *is* nice. But why? Why do you love having me as your father?"

William ponders and then responds, "Well, because we get to have tea together in this grand palace waited on by all these servants. And I get to own the Duchy of Cornwall and make a splendid living off all of its proceeds. Everyone calls me prince and bows down before me. And one day, because you're my dad, all of this will be mine! All mine!"

That would be just awful, wouldn't it? But why? Because Prince William would be entirely focused on all the benefits he receives as the king's son rather than on the king himself.

Think for a moment about how you describe your identity as a Christian. Often we speak about being forgiven or justified. Sometimes we say that we have been redeemed or reconciled. We might even say that we have been made holy or adopted into God's family. All of those things are wonderfully true, but they are the benefits of the gospel rather than the gospel itself. They are the gifts rather than the Giver. The good news of the gospel is that the Giver of gifts has given us himself. That is how the distinct yet inseparable relationship between God and his people is restored.

The very first sin involved a tragic separation of the Giver from the gift. In Genesis 2, God showed himself to be lavishly generous. He gave every tree in the garden to Adam and Eve for food—every tree but one. When the serpent arrived in Genesis 3, his first move was to lie, leading Eve to focus on the gifts rather than the Giver.[6] He questioned God's generosity and pointed Adam and Eve to the one thing God did not give them. In so doing, he blinded Adam and Eve to the supreme gift: the gift of God himself,

---

6. This, of course, was all part of Satan's ploy to get Eve to desire autonomy—to be "like God" in determining good and evil (Gen. 3:5).

who dwelt with them in the garden. That is how sin came into the world—through separating the Giver and the gift and making humanity believe that they could possess God's gifts independently of him.

In understanding our identity as Christians, we must grasp that the greatest gift of the gospel is that God gives himself. The good news is that we get God. And in getting God, we get every spiritual blessing in him, which is the topic of the next chapter.

Living It Out: Relationship, Not Religion

Twenty-first-century Western society is heavily transactional. We're trained from the earliest age to assume that if we work hard at school, we will do well on our exams and get a good job. If we are polite and friendly, people will like us, and we will have lots of good friends. If we eat well and exercise daily, we will be fit and healthy, and all will go well. Our natural assumption is that if we *do* something, certain results will follow. This is why religion, when defined as *doing* things to earn God's favor, is so appealing. It resonates with our transactional understanding of life.

But at the heart of the gospel is relationship with God, not a works-based religion. As we saw in part 2, it is about how God has repaired our distinct yet inseparable relationship with him, not how we bargain for our salvation with God.

I remember very well my first visit to East Africa. We woke up on the first morning, had breakfast, and waited outside the hostel for our coach to arrive. We had been told that the coach would be there by 9 a.m., but an hour passed, and then another, with no sign of the promised transportation. It was shortly before lunch when the coach finally arrived.

One of my party asked the driver what had happened, expecting him to relay an excuse about how the coach had blown a tire or had been involved in an accident. Instead, the driver just shrugged his shoulders and said that he had run into a friend on his way into work and lost track of the time.

While Western culture tends to be task-oriented, East African culture is much more people-oriented and relational. We have much to learn from our East African brothers and sisters when it comes to how we relate to God. It is not that we do nothing as Christians—Jesus calls on us to be very active, after all. Nor is it true that we receive nothing from God, as we will see in the next chapter. The point is that the Christian life and Christian identity are first and foremost about relationship with God, not works done to confirm salvation. Like Martha, we need to learn to be with Jesus and listen to him (see Luke 10:38–43).

Making It Personal

1. Can you recall a time when you were tempted to rely on your own actions as a source of assurance of salvation? Why did you do this?
2. How often do you think about your identity as being "in Christ"? Where else do you look for your identity, and why is this problematic?
3. Why do you think the Roman Catholic Church's doctrine of grace became so popular? What makes it appealing?
4. Do you tend to view God in transactional or relational terms? Why? How can you focus on your relationship with him as your supreme blessing?
5. In what ways can you see a transactional approach to God affecting the church?
6. How might you focus on the Giver rather than his gifts in your prayers? In your worship? In your witness and your conversations with others? If you are studying this book in a group, take time to pray for one another as you seek to focus on the Giver.

11

GOSPEL GIFTS

> *The gospel gifts of justification, sanctification, and adoption are distinct because justification and adoption are declarative, while sanctification involves inward change. The gifts are, however, inseparable because you cannot be justified without also being sanctified and adopted.*

Paul opens his letter to the Ephesians with these words: "Praise be to the God and Father of our Lord Jesus Christ, who has blessed us in the heavenly realms with every spiritual blessing in Christ" (Eph. 1:3). We receive every spiritual blessing—every gift—in Christ. In this chapter, we will focus on three gospel gifts and see how they are received distinctly but inseparably from one another through our union with Christ.

Three Gifts

Justification

John Calvin described justification as "the main hinge on which religion turns."[1] Some say, "Justification means God views me 'just as if I'd never sinned.'" That is a helpful way to remember part of what justification involves,

---

1. John Calvin, *Institutes of the Christian Religion*, ed. John T. McNeill, trans. Ford Lewis Battles (Philadelphia: Westminster John Knox Press, 1960), 3.11.1.

but it is inadequate. The word in the original Greek is *dikaios*, and its root means "righteous." So, to justify someone is to "righteous" them. Justification is not only "as if you had never sinned"; it is also "as if you are entirely righteous." But what does this mean?

The earliest example of justification in the Bible comes in Genesis 15. Abram fears that the four kings he's just defeated might return to get revenge. The Lord assures Abram that he is Abram's shield and his very great reward. He then reiterates his promise to give Abram more descendants than he can possibly number. After this, we read that "Abram believed the Lord, and he credited it to him as righteousness" (Gen. 15:6). God justified (credited righteousness to) Abram on account of his faith. Paul explains this in Romans 4:5: "To the one who does not work but trusts God who justifies the ungodly, their faith is credited as righteousness."

Justification by faith lies at the heart of the gospel. In Romans 3:25–26, Paul writes,

> God presented Christ as a sacrifice of atonement, through the shedding of his blood—to be received by faith. He did this to demonstrate his righteousness, because in his forbearance he had left the sins committed beforehand unpunished—he did it to demonstrate his righteousness at the present time, so as to be just and the one who justifies those who have faith in Jesus.

It is important to notice what exactly is happening here. As we have seen, the word translated "righteousness" and the word translated "justifies" both have the same root in the original Greek. Jesus's death on the cross achieved two outcomes related to justice:

1. It demonstrated God's justice—his everlasting righteousness. In the past, God had left sins unpunished, but on the cross he punished the sins of all believers, past, present, and future. The cross vindicated God's perfect justice because it paid for past sins as well as present and future sins.
2. It credited (or imputed) Christ's righteousness to sinners. The Reformer Martin Luther called this the "sweet exchange" and

encouraged Christians to pray in this way: "You, Lord Jesus, are my righteousness and I am your sin. You have taken on yourself what you were not, and have given to me what I am not."[2]

To understand the nature of justification and the sweet exchange that took place on the cross, it is important to distinguish between two types of action: a declarative act and a transformative act.

To illustrate the difference, consider what I used to do when I was a law lecturer. I spent most of my year teaching students in lectures and tutorials. Those were transformative acts. I was sharing knowledge and helping students think critically about the law. Their brains were being filled with legal precedents, and their minds were being shaped to think like a lawyer. My acts were changing them. I was infusing knowledge and skill—or trying to!

At the end of the year, however, we would have a big ceremony. The chancellor of the university would attend, there would be speeches, and then each student would file to the front and receive a graduation certificate. That certificate confirmed that they had passed their exams and were ready for the next step of legal training. It was a declarative act.

As we saw in the previous chapter, the Roman Catholic Church teaches that justification is a transformative act: God infuses his righteousness into us through the seven sacraments, and we cooperate with that righteousness in the hope that, on the day of judgment, we might receive final justification.

However, the Bible's description of justification is very different. It teaches that justification is a legal declaration by God that proclaims the opposite of condemnation (see 1 Kings 8:32; Matt. 12:37; Rom. 5:16; 8:33–34). In justification, God declares that a person is free from the penalty of sin (see Rom. 4:6–8; 8:1) *and* completely righteous in his sight (see Isa. 61:10; Rom. 4:3; 5:19).

This declaration changes the legal relationship between us and God and constitutes a new reality. As Calvin wrote, "He is justified who is reckoned in the condition not of a sinner, but of a righteous man; and for that reason, he

---

2. Martin Luther, *Luther's Works*, vol. 48, *Letters I*, ed. Jaroslav Pelikan, Helmut T. Lehmann, and Christopher Boyd Brown (Philadelphia: Fortress Press, 1955), 12.

stands firm before God's judgment seat while all sinners fall."[3] Justification is a settled state that is totally certain because it depends on Christ's past work. It is a cause for great joy and thankfulness in the Christian.

Sanctification

The second spiritual blessing that we will consider is sanctification. The English word *sanctification* comes from the Latin verb *sanctificare*, which is a combination of two Latin words: *sanctus*, meaning "holy," and *facere*, meaning "to make." The word translates a Hebrew word, *qadosh*, and a Greek word, *hagiasmos*, both of which operate in the same way, having "holiness" as their root.

The word *holy* is a bit difficult to define. In some places, it is used to describe God himself. For example, in Isaiah 6, the prophet Isaiah sees the Lord seated in his throne room, surrounded by angels who call out to one another, "Holy, holy, holy is the Lord Almighty" (v. 3). In this context, the word *holy* is being used almost as an adjective for God, referring back to his exaltation and righteousness (see 5:16). He is the thrice holy God—God, God, God—and therefore worthy of the angels' praise.

In other places, the word *holy* is used to describe things that are dedicated or sanctified to God. For example, in 1 Kings 7:51, Solomon brings "the things his father David had dedicated [*qadosh*]"—gold, silver, and other articles—into the temple. The Lord also sanctifies people. In Leviticus 20:26, God declares, "You are to be holy [*qadosh*] to me because I, the Lord, am holy, and I have set you apart from the nations to be my own." Here, the Lord is almost "godding" the people of Israel. He is not making them gods, but he is declaring them to be his own and separating them to be his holy people.

Once we reach the New Testament, we discover that all Christians are sanctified (although not yet perfected—see chapter 12) and are repeatedly called "holy" or "saints" (same root word). Paul describes the church in Rome as "loved by God and called to be his holy people" (Rom. 1:7). In 1 Corinthians 1:2, he describes the church as "those sanctified in Christ Jesus and called to be his holy people." He defines the church in Ephesus as "God's holy people

---

3. Calvin, *Institutes*, 3.11.2.

in Ephesus" (Eph. 1:1) and the believers in Philippi as "God's holy people in Christ Jesus at Philippi" (Phil. 1:1). All Christians are holy people—saints—a status they receive by virtue of being "in Christ Jesus." This is in stark contrast to the Roman Catholic doctrines of beatification and canonization, whereby sainthood is something bestowed on a limited number of believers by the Pope.

Unlike justification, sanctification is a transformative act. The clue is in the Latin word from which it is derived—it means "make holy," not "count holy" or "declare holy." Sanctification is a change that we actually experience. Those who are in Christ are not merely declared to be holy but are made holy—"godded"—transformed into Christ's likeness. We will return to this subject in the next chapter.

Adoption

The third spiritual gift we will examine is adoption. This is a declarative act of God by which he makes us members of his family. In Roman law, a childless adult could adopt a male as his son in order to continue his family line. The heir would not normally be chosen until he was an adult so that the adoptive parent could thoroughly assess him and ensure that he was worthy to receive the honor and the inheritance.

The glorious good news is that God chose to adopt us while we were utterly unworthy. Paul writes, "God sent his Son, born of a woman, born under the law, to redeem those under the law, that we might receive adoption to sonship" (Gal. 4:4–5). God's choice was motivated not by our merit but by his own love: "In love he predestined us for adoption to sonship through Jesus Christ, in accordance with his pleasure and will—to the praise of his glorious grace" (Eph. 1:4–6).

English theologian J. I. Packer describes adoption as the "highest privilege that the gospel offers." He continues, "Adoption is a *family* idea, conceived in terms of *love*, and viewing God as *father*. In adoption, God takes us into his family and fellowship, and establishes us as his children and heirs. Closeness, affection and generosity are at the heart of the relationship."[4] Adoption involves an incredible change of status. We were "children of wrath"

---

4. J. I. Packer, *Knowing God* (London: Hodder & Stoughton, 1998), 187–88. Emphasis in original.

(Eph. 2:3 ESV) and children of the devil (see John 8:44), but we have been made "sons of God" (Rom. 8:14 ESV). Adoption is a declarative act that is tied closely to redemption. It is the purpose of our redemption—that is, we have been redeemed from slavery (see Rom. 8:15) in order to be sons of God (see Gal. 4:4–5).

Justification Adoption	Sanctification
Declarative	**Transformative**

Fig. 11.1. Aspects of Union with Christ

Distinct but Inseparable

Throughout church history, much error and confusion have been caused either by mixing these three gospel gifts or by separating them from one another. In the section that follows, we will examine these two errors. We will then see how the Bible presents the three gifts as being received distinctly but inseparably from one another through our union with Christ.

Inseparable but Not Distinct

We have already looked at the Roman Catholic teaching on grace, which views grace as a substance transferred through the sacraments and combined with our own good works to form the basis of our justification. The fundamental error of this view is that it mixes sanctification with justification. In this case, God's declaration that believers have right standing with him is made dependent on the transformative act of sanctification.

The sixteenth-century Roman Catholic Council of Trent explicitly acknowledged this conflation of justification and sanctification when it declared that the efficient cause of justification "is a merciful God who washes and sanctifies gratuitously."[5] Roman Catholics believe that God's

---

5. Council of Trent, Session 6.7. The efficient cause means the "agent of change."

judgment on the last day will be based on the fruits of our sanctification rather than on Christ's finished work on our behalf. According to this understanding, a believer can never really know whether their salvation is secure.

Indeed, assurance of salvation is viewed as a vice, not a virtue, in official Roman Catholic teaching. Canon XII of the Council of Trent states, "If any one saith, that justifying faith is nothing else but confidence in the divine mercy which remits sins for Christ's sake . . . let him be anathema." This utterly undermines a Christian's eternal security and makes their identity constantly subject to change.

Justification
Sanctification

Fig. 11.2. Roman Catholic View—Indistinct and Inseparable

The Reformers rejected this understanding of the relationship between justification and sanctification and insisted that Scripture clearly distinguishes between the two gospel gifts. Justification, according to Scripture, is always legal and declarative. Believers are *counted* righteous because of what *Christ* has done, not because of any righteousness in themselves. Indeed, this is why the apostle Paul spoke of "one who does not work but trusts God who justifies the ungodly" (Rom. 4:5), and why Martin Luther famously described believers as being *simul iustus et peccator*—at the same time righteous and a sinner.

Justification deals with the problem of a person's legal guilt, while sanctification addresses a person's moral pollution. Sanctification is a transformative act resulting in an actual change in the person's internal condition before God, while justification is a forensic (legal) and declarative act producing no inner transformation. According to the Reformers, Rome's error was that it eroded the distinction between these two gospel gifts.

Distinct and Separate

It is important, however, that we do not fall into the opposite error of entirely separating justification and sanctification. The Roman church accused the Reformers of this error and said that it would lead to antinomianism (meaning anti-law), whereby Christians would carry on sinning because they believed that they were saved by faith alone and therefore that they did not need to grow in holiness.

Justification   Sanctification

Fig. 11.3. Antinomian Protestant View—Distinct and Separate

The Reformers responded by saying that they were teaching nothing of the sort. The seventeenth-century theologian Francis Turretin, for example, insisted that the Reformers spoke with one voice as they taught "that the benefits of justification and sanctification are so *indissolubly connected* [inseparable] with each other that God justifies no one without equally sanctifying him and giving inherent righteousness by the creating of a new man in true righteousness and holiness."[6] In other words, justification and sanctification are distinct but inseparable gospel gifts that flow to the believer from the completed work of Christ. You cannot have justification without sanctification because both necessarily result from our union with Christ.

Is there some order to the gospel gifts, however? In the sixteenth century, William Perkins produced an illustration that sought to show how God works in salvation. He called it "The Golden Chaine of Salvation." Down the center of his diagram, Perkins placed the work of Christ, and alongside this he put the experience of the believer—in which justification is followed by sanctification and ends with glorification.

6. Francis Turretin, *Institutes of Elenctic Theology*, ed. James T. Dennison Jr., trans. George Musgrave Giger (Phillipsburg, NJ: P&R Publishing, 1994), 16.2.4 (emphasis added).

```
┌─────────────────┐
│    Election     │
└─────────────────┘
         ∨
┌─────────────────┐
│    Calling      │
└─────────────────┘
         ∨
┌─────────────────┐
│  Justification  │
└─────────────────┘
         ∨
┌─────────────────┐
│  Sanctification │
└─────────────────┘
         ∨
┌─────────────────┐
│  Glorification  │
└─────────────────┘
```

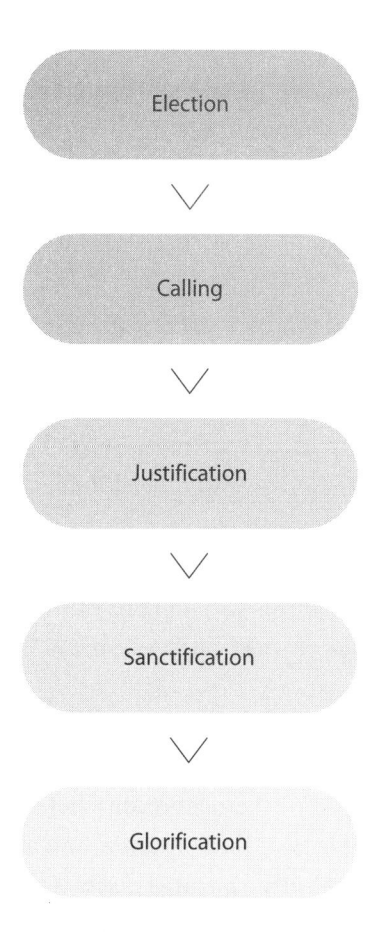

Fig. 11.4. Golden Chain of Salvation (Simplified)

Perkins was clear that all these gospel gifts were tied to Christ's work, but the chain implied a logical order to the gifts. Over time, Perkins's chain became very popular, and people began to talk about the temporal and logical order of the gospel gifts. This had the effect of improperly separating the gifts—justification was viewed as what has happened to believers in the past, sanctification as what is happening to believers in the present, and adoption as the Christian's hope for the future.

Does this logical separation of the gifts really matter? I believe that it does, as it has significant implications for how we understand the Christian life. When I was a young Christian, I was told by a well-meaning pastor that justification is the fuel for our sanctification. "What you need to understand," he said, "is that we have been declared righteous in Christ [justification]. Our role is now to live it out [sanctification]. Be who God has declared you to be."

There are a number of problems with this teaching. First, it turns justification into a cosmic visual aid. Justification becomes a legal fiction—we are counted righteous, though we are not actually righteous—that inspires us to pursue holiness.

Second, it emphasizes our own participation in the work of sanctification. We are to pull up our socks and become how God sees us in Christ. The Holy Spirit will help us, but sanctification does not involve a radical change in who we are. As we will see in the next chapter, there is so much more to sanctification than this, and indeed it *does* involve an immediate and radical change in who we are.

Third, the teaching disconnects the gospel gifts (sanctification and justification) from Christ. Instead of looking to Christ for our sanctification, we look to the visual aid of justification—a benefit of Christ rather than Christ himself.

Distinct but Inseparable

The Bible's description of the relationship between the gospel gifts is radically different. Justification, sanctification, and adoption are presented as three aspects of our union with Christ, each of which is ours distinctly and inseparably through our union with Christ.

See how the apostle Paul puts it in 1 Corinthians 1:30: "It is because of him that you are in Christ Jesus, who has become for us wisdom from God—that is, our righteousness, holiness and redemption." The last part of that verse could be translated "that is, our justification, sanctification and redemption"; they are the same words in the Greek. Christ Jesus has been sent from God the Father to be our justification, sanctification, and redemption. Remember, redemption is for the purpose of adoption: we have been set free (redeemed) for sonship (adoption). This means that our adoption is not founded on our sanctification. Nor is our sanctification founded on or fueled by our justification. All three gifts have their foundation in our union with Christ and are received the very moment we are united to him —distinctly and inseparably.

Living It Out: A Given and Experienced Identity

What we have seen in this chapter has important implications for our understanding of our own identity as Christians. In ancient times, people found their identity—their place in the world—in their families, their social class, and their vocations. A young man would be called James Johnson not because Johnson is a great name (although I do like it) but because he was James, son of John. The Baker family were called Bakers because, for ten generations, they had worked as bakers. The Butchers, Carpenters, Farmers, and Smiths were all given their surnames because of what they *did*.

For millennia, people's identities were rooted in factors almost entirely outside their control. Had Wolfgang Amadeus Mozart been born to a British butcher rather than a German composer, he might well have invented an interesting new sausage, but we would not have been blessed by his *Requiem* or his *Clarinet Concerto*. Composing music for a living would almost certainly have been beyond his grasp, regardless of the amount of musical talent with which he was born.

The past century has seen a fundamental reframing of the concept of identity. The American political scientist Francis Fukuyama writes of this change, "Individuals [have] come to believe that they have a true or authentic identity hiding within themselves that is somehow at odds with the role they are assigned by their surrounding society. The modern concept of identity places a supreme value on authenticity, on the validation of that inner being that is not being allowed to express itself. It is on the side of the inner and not the outer self."[7] In contemporary thinking, identity is internal rather than external. It is discovered rather than assigned, and it is subject to constant change as we repeatedly ask ourselves the question, "Who am I, really?"

In recent times, this has been particularly pronounced in the realm of gender. Our society has dislocated biological sex and gender and actively encourages individuals (including children) to discover the gender within themselves rather than embracing the gender assigned to them at birth. We will explore this in greater detail in chapter 16.

---

7. Francis Fukuyama, *Identity: The Demand for Dignity and the Politics of Resentment* (London: Profile Books, 2018), 25.

Where does the Christian stand? Is our identity fundamentally external or internal? Is it something that we are given or something that we discover or create for ourselves? Does our identity change? As we saw in chapter 4, our natural identity is something that is both assigned to us and present within us. Our surname at birth should be Adam. We are born in his sin and separation from God, which are internalized by the natural bent of our hearts. As Augustine famously said, we are *incurvatus in se*—curved in on ourselves. But, thanks to the gospel, we have been given a new identity. We now carry the surname Christ. We are in him, and he is in us. What is his is ours; what happened to him has also happened to us.

This means, on the one hand, that our identity is something that is external and assigned—Martin Luther said that Christians have an external, or "alien," righteousness in Christ.[8] On the other hand, however, our new identity is fundamentally internal as well. Christ now dwells in us by the Spirit, and alongside the declarations of justification and adoption we also have the inner transformation of sanctification.

The answer to the question "Who am I, really?" has changed and should continue to change. We are a "new creation" (2 Cor. 5:17); we become more human than we have ever been as we grow into the likeness of the resurrected Christ. Our identity in Christ is something to be discovered and explored as we enjoy the fruits of our union with Christ day by day. This gives believers the sort of confidence, contentment, and security that our society craves and should spur us on to share Christ with our friends, family, and colleagues. It really is good news for a culture paralyzed by identity crisis.

Making It Personal

1. Which of the following are you tempted to believe?
    - Antinomianism, or cheap grace: "I'm saved, so God will forgive me, no matter what I do . . . so I can live how I want!"
    - Legalism, or salvation by works: "I must prove myself to God —otherwise, I'm not sure if I'll be saved!"

---

8. Martin Luther, "Sermon on Two Kinds of Righteousness," in *The Annotated Luther*, vol. 2, *Word and Faith*, ed. Kirsi I. Stjerna (Philadelphia: Fortress Press, 2015), 13.

2. How does Scripture confront both extremes?
3. How do you tend to separate the gospel gifts from our union with Christ? In what ways does this hamper you from worshipping Christ and pursuing godliness?
4. How could seeing your identity in Christ as both externally assigned and internally discovered and explored help you
   - understand your true identity;
   - deal with disappointment and failure;
   - grow as a Christian;
   - fight sin;
   - share the gospel in a culture paralyzed by identity crisis; and
   - disciple Christians in a culture where identity is plastic?

12

PAST, PRESENT, AND FUTURE

> *The gift of sanctification involves real and immediate transformation that fuels the Christian life. In Christ, we are given the identity and the recognition that we long for.*

As we have seen, one of the mistakes of "golden chaine" thinking is that it arranges the gospel gifts in a temporal order: we are justified in the past, sanctified in the present, and adopted in the future. When we examine the Scriptures, however, we discover that all three gospel gifts have a past, present, and future orientation because they are all founded on our union with Christ, which itself has a past, present, and future orientation. We will begin with justification and adoption, as they are more straightforward, and then dive into sanctification.

Justification: Past, Present, and Future

Let's look at justification first. It is clear that justification has a past orientation—we *have been* justified through our union with Christ, who bore our sin on the cross (see Rom. 3:24, 5:1). It is also clear that we have a present status as justified people—here and now, we are covered by Christ's righteousness (see Rom. 5:9). The Bible also teaches that justification has a future orientation. In Galatians 5:5, for instance, Paul writes, "Through the

Spirit we eagerly await by faith the righteousness [justification] for which we hope." This looks toward the future day of judgment, when our past verdict of "justified" will be confirmed as we stand in Christ before God's judgment seat.

Adoption: Past, Present, and Future

Similarly, adoption has a past, present, and future orientation. In eternity past, God "predestined us for adoption to sonship" (Eph. 1:5). We now enjoy the blessings of adoption as the Holy Spirit testifies "with our spirit that we are God's children" (Rom. 8:16). But adoption also has a future orientation. A little later in his letter to the Romans, Paul writes that we "groan inwardly as we wait eagerly for our adoption to sonship, the redemption of our bodies" (8:23). This shows that adoption and glorification are inextricably linked. Because we are already adopted, we will be perfectly transformed (future glorification) when Christ returns and will bear the family likeness as children of God.

Sanctification: Past, Present, and Future

Sanctification also has three orientations. People sometimes contrast justification with sanctification, saying that justification is a single act in the past, while sanctification is an ongoing process in the present. It is true (as we have seen) that justification is a single act with past, present, and future consequences. It is also true that sanctification is an ongoing process, but it is much more than that. In fact, sanctification begins and ends with single acts, and the ongoing process is what lies between the two.

Past: Definitive Sanctification

The single act at the start of sanctification is sometimes referred to as *definitive sanctification*. When the New Testament discusses sanctification, this is usually what it means. We have already looked at 1 Corinthians 1:2, where the apostle Paul describes the church in Corinth as "sanctified in Christ Jesus." He uses the perfect tense of the verb to indicate that the Corinthians are already in a "state" of sanctification. It is not a process—at least not in this instance.

A bit later, in 1 Corinthians 6, Paul presents a long list of what the Corinthians once were (idolaters, adulterers, thieves, drunkards, and so on), after which he writes, "But you were washed, you were sanctified, you were justified in the name of the Lord Jesus Christ and by the Spirit of our God" (v. 11). Notice what Paul does here: he lists sanctification and justification as single, definitive acts that happened the very moment the Corinthians put their trust in Christ.

In this verse, the tense form of both Greek verbs ("were sanctified," "were justified") is aorist, which is a snapshot tense, like a camera taking a picture. It describes an action that has happened in a specific moment in time. These verbs are also in the passive voice, which means that justification and sanctification, in this context, are things that were *done to* the Corinthian believers rather than *done by* them. Paul is saying, in effect, "You have been made holy, and you are now living in a state of holiness."

Now, what exactly is definitive sanctification? The fullest explanation is found in Romans 6. To understand Paul's teaching, it is important to realize that he is almost personifying sin in this chapter. He describes sin as a ruling power that enslaves us. Before we put our trust in Christ, we cannot help but sin. As Paul writes,

> For we know that our old self was crucified with him [Christ] so that the body ruled by sin might be done away with, that we should no longer be slaves to sin—because anyone who has died has been set free from sin. Now if we died with Christ, we believe that we will also live with him. For we know that since Christ was raised from the dead, he cannot die again; death no longer has mastery over him. The death he died, he died to sin once for all; but the life he lives, he lives to God. (vv. 6–10)

What Paul says in these verses is simply stunning. Through faith, we have been united to Christ in his death, which means that our body that was once ruled by sin has been "done away with" (v. 6). We are no longer slaves to sin. We have been freed from its rule.

And notice the reason Paul gives for our freedom in verse 10: "The death he [Christ] died, he died to sin." At first glance, that may seem confusing. Surely Jesus was sinless. What does it mean that he died to sin? We need to remember that sin, in this context, is portrayed as a ruling power. As we saw in part 2, Jesus took on a fully human nature when he was born into the "old age." He experienced pain, suffering, grief, and temptation. In a very real sense, he was born under the power of sin. Unlike us, however, he said no to sin, and through his death, he and we have victory over the enslaving power of sin.

Remember that death is all about separation. Those united to Christ have been forever separated from the ruling power of sin. Sin is like a person who is always calling out to us. In the past, we were chained to sin, and sin could pull us closer and closer—ultimately, there was nothing we could do to escape its lure. In our union with Christ, however, the chain to sin has been broken, and sin is no longer inevitable for Christians. That is definitive sanctification.

Definitive Sanctification

Free from slavery to sin

Past

Fig. 12.1. Past Orientation of Sanctification

Present: Progressive Sanctification

Sin remains in the world, however. It calls out to us in temptation, which is why sanctification is also an ongoing process for the believer. We see this as we continue reading Romans 6. Paul instructs the Roman believers to "count yourselves dead to sin but alive to God in Christ Jesus" (v. 11). "Recognize what has happened to you," Paul says, "and live it out." We do not simply have a new standing before God (justification); we also have a new nature (sanctification) that we must live out.

There's a story about the fourth-century bishop Augustine. In his early years, Augustine was a rogue who slept around with many different women. Later in his life, after he'd become a Christian, Augustine was walking through a city when one of his former mistresses saw him. She came over and struck up conversation with him, but she noticed that his demeanor seemed different. He was cordial, but he didn't talk like he used to. Eventually he broke off the conversation and moved on down the street. The woman was perplexed, and then it dawned on her: "Perhaps he didn't recognize me." So she yelled out, "Augustine, it is I." Augustine turned to her and replied, "Yes, but it isn't I!" This is what Paul is telling Christians to do in verse 11.

We must constantly remind ourselves that we are changed people. The ruling power of sin has been broken in our lives, and we are no longer slaves to it. Progressive sanctification also involves actively throwing sin out of our lives (see Rom. 6:12) and using our bodies for holy ends rather than sinful ones (see v. 13). It is an active process of becoming more and more like Christ, enabled by the Holy Spirit. The imperatives (the "do") of progressive sanctification follow and are fueled by the indicatives (the "done") of definitive sanctification.

Definitive Sanctification	Progressive Sanctification
Free from slavery to sin	Battling sin and becoming like Christ
Past	Present

Fig. 12.2. Past and Present Orientations of Sanctification

Future: Perfect Sanctification

Progressive sanctification ultimately points forward to a future sanctification, where we will be perfected—made like Christ. The ruling power of sin has been broken in the past (definitive sanctification). We are battling sin in the present (progressive sanctification). One day, sin itself will be expunged, and we will be made perfectly like Christ (perfect sanctification). John describes this amazing day in his first letter: "But we know that when Christ appears, we shall be like him, for we shall see him as he is" (1 John 3:2).

That is the future for Christians. In an instant, we will be transformed into the perfect holiness of Christ. What a day that will be!

Definitive Sanctification	Progressive Sanctification	Perfect Sanctification
Free from slavery to sin	Battling sin and becoming like Christ	Forever free of the presence of sin and made perfect like Christ
Past	Present	Future

Fig. 12.3. Past, Present, and Future Orientations of Sanctification

Living It Out: The Fight with Sin Is Winnable

Back in chapter 11, I recalled how a well-meaning pastor had once told me that my justification was the fuel for my sanctification. The pastor was saying, in essence, "The gospel is the good news that God looks at you and sees Christ. Now live up to that!" It's like being told, "Your father got straight As in school, and so did your grandfather. Now it's your turn!" It's a crushing burden. And it is not the gospel.

God didn't only declare us righteous in Christ—he *made* us holy in Christ too. The gospel gifts are both declarative (justification and adoption) and transformative (sanctification). If we are united to Christ, the ruling power of sin has been broken in our lives. We are new creations.

Pause to consider what this means. There is now no temptation, no battle with sin, no struggle with our old self, that Christians are not equipped to win. We have a divine armory that is more than sufficient to fight whatever the world, the flesh, or the devil may throw at us. Sin is no longer inevitable for you if you are a Christian.

Now, this is not to say that we *won't* sin. John is clear about this: "If we claim to be without sin, we deceive ourselves and the truth is not in us" (1 John 1:8). This side of Christ's return, every Christian will sin. But three verses later, John writes, "My dear children, I write this to you so that you will not sin" (2:1).

We will face the temptation to sin every day. Some of us will battle greed; others will fight against lust or laziness; still others will war against gossip. Before we were united to Christ, sin was inevitable in each of those areas. We couldn't help but sin. But not anymore! We have died with Christ to the ruling power of greed, lust, sloth, and slander. We have the power to say no. This side of Christ's return, we will not always resist sin, but each day is a new day and one on which we must remind ourselves that we have died to sin and now live to God (see Rom. 6:10).

The Good News Is That We Get Christ

Let us tie together everything we have seen in part 4. The good news of the gospel is that we get Christ. Grace is not a thing that is infused into us; grace is God's unmerited favor, received by us in a person: Jesus. All this means that Jesus himself is the supreme gift of the gospel. All the other gospel gifts are just aspects or benefits of our union with Christ, and we cannot receive any of those things without first receiving Christ.

No one has put it better than John Calvin in the introduction to book 3 of his *Institutes of the Christian Religion*: "We must understand that as long as Christ remains outside of us, and we are separated from him, all that he has suffered and done for the salvation of the human race remains useless and of no value for us. Therefore, to share with us what he has received from the Father, he had to become ours and to dwell within us."[1]

There are no gospel gifts apart from *the* gospel gift of Jesus Christ, received through union with him by Spirit-enabled faith. And if we do receive him, we will enjoy all his benefits as well. Again, Calvin explains it much better than I can: "Christ was given to us by God's generosity, to be grasped and possessed by us in faith. By partaking of him, we principally receive a double grace: namely, that being reconciled to God through Christ's blamelessness, we may have in heaven instead of a Judge a gracious Father; and secondly, that sanctified by Christ's spirit we may cultivate blamelessness and purity of life."[2]

---

1. John Calvin, *Institutes of the Christian Religion*, ed. John T. McNeill, trans. Ford Lewis Battles (Philadelphia: Westminster John Knox Press, 1960), 3.1.1.
2. Calvin, 3.11.1.

In Christ we receive justification, sanctification, and adoption distinctly but inseparably from one another. Two important conclusions follow from this. First, the benefits of union with Christ are founded on and rooted in Christ and his finished work, not in one another. They are distinct. This means that justification is not the fuel for sanctification and that sanctification is not the route to adoption. All three are received as distinct benefits through union with Christ.

Second, and no less important, the benefits of union with Christ are inseparable. You cannot have one without the others. If you are justified, then you are also sanctified and adopted. That is why the apostle Paul could reply, "By no means!" to the question "Shall we go on sinning so that grace may increase?" (Rom. 6:2, 1). If we have died with Christ to the penalty of sin (justification), we have also died with Christ to the ruling power of sin (sanctification). A Christian is a justified and holy child of God.

Living It Out: Recognition

In his book *Identity*, Francis Fukuyama discusses the three parts of the soul as described by the philosopher Plato in his work *Republic*. One part of the soul, the *eros*, is concerned with desire—it thirsts, hungers, wants. The second part, the *logos*, is concerned with reason—it thinks and calculates, which leads to conflicts with the *eros* when one's desires are not in one's best interest. Plato called the third part of the soul *thymos*. This part judges worth—it is the part of you that seeks recognition.

Fukuyama writes, "Human beings do not just want things that are external to themselves, such as food, drink, Lamborghinis, or that next hit. They also crave positive judgments about their worth and dignity."[3] He suggests that this is what drives contemporary identity politics. People crave positive external affirmation of their internal self-identity. It is not enough for people to simply discover who they are; they need the surrounding society to recognize and celebrate it too.

---

3. Francis Fukuyama, *Identity: The Demand for Dignity and the Politics of Resentment* (London: Profile Books, 2018), 18.

This theme is endlessly played out in contemporary literature and film because it resonates so deeply. For example, in the first *Rocky* film, on the night before his big fight with Apollo Creed, Rocky discusses the fight with his wife: "All I wanna do is go the distance.... And if I can go that distance and that bell rings and I'm still standin', I'm gonna know for the first time in my life, see, that I weren't just another bum from the neighborhood." That is how many of us live our lives—desperate for success in school, sports, work, and love so that we can prove we're not a bum.

For Christians, our distinct but inseparable identity in Christ meets this desire for recognition while staying true to who we are. The external affirmation that we crave has already been given. We are justified in Christ, which is distinct from his ongoing work in our lives: sanctification. This means that whether I have a really good day or an absolutely terrible day, the verdict is exactly the same. I am not a bum. I am righteous.

And even more wonderfully, I am loved. In Christ, we have the distinct but inseparable gift of adoption. Whether we are homeless or wealthy, the most important recognition we could possibly receive has already been bestowed on us. We have been made dearly loved children of God.

We must not keep this good news to ourselves. We live in a culture where people are desperately seeking an identity that is concrete, externally affirmed, and inwardly felt. Tragically, people look for this by aligning themselves with group identifies that are essentially negative—defined by what they oppose.

Take, for example, Marxist politics, in its separation of the bourgeoisie from the proletariat, or transgender ideology, in its separation of transgender from cisgender (a person whose gender identity corresponds with their sex assigned at birth). Although these group identities offer external affirmation and a degree of inward experience, they divide rather than unite, and they are forever subject to change and loss as circumstances and experiences vary. They do not provide the concrete identity or the unity in diversity that the world craves. Only our immutable identity in Christ can provide that.

Making It Personal

1. What comfort, hope, or joy is there in knowing that you are united to Christ today?

2. What aspects of justification, sanctification, and adoption do you struggle most to remember or live out? Why do you think that is?
3. In what areas of your life do you need to remind yourself that you are dead to sin but alive to God in Christ Jesus? How can you do this? What help might you need?
4. Do you look forward to your future and perfect sanctification? Why or why not?
5. Do you crave recognition? In what areas do you see that desire driving your thoughts, words, and actions?
6. How could dwelling on the inseparable yet distinct benefits of your union with Christ help you recognize your true identity? How could it help you hold out that hope to others who don't yet know Christ?
7. Pray for an opportunity this week to share with an unbeliever the joys of finding your identity and recognition in Christ.

Further Reading for Part 4

DeYoung, Kevin. *The Hole in our Holiness: Filling the Gap between Gospel Passion and the Pursuit of Godliness*. Wheaton, IL: Crossway, 2012.

Ferguson, Sinclair B. *The Whole Christ: Legalism, Antinomianism, and Gospel Assurance—Why the Marrow Controversy Still Matters*. Wheaton, IL: Crossway, 2016.

Murray, John. *Redemption Accomplished and Applied*. Grand Rapids: Eerdmans, 2015.

Packer, J. I. *Knowing God*. London: Hodder & Stoughton, 1998.

Part 5

How Does a Christian Grow?

Have you ever longed for a "silver bullet" to solve your problems? As I write this chapter, I've been helping my son, Jacob, prepare for his 11+ exam, a test taken in the UK just before applying to high school. Parents spend thousands preparing their children for the test—buying books, hiring tutors, and so on. They are looking for a "silver bullet"—a magic key—to 11+ success. Whether it be passing exams, finding a spouse, parenting, or buying a house, we are always looking for silver bullets.

It is easy to bring that desire into the Christian life. Surely there must be a silver bullet that produces exponential growth in godliness, a way to connect with the Spirit that guarantees immediate blessing and spiritual growth. In 2000, Bruce Wilkinson published a book titled *The Prayer of Jabez*, which claimed to reveal a secret method for "breaking through to the blessed life." It was one of many attempts to identify the key to connecting with the Spirit, defeating sin, and experiencing astonishing spiritual growth.

I'm going to let you in on a secret of my own . . . I've found the key. Actually, it's not a secret because the church has been using this key for thousands of years. Nor is it a silver bullet, because if you're going to use it rightly, it will require a lot of hard work, perseverance, and faith. But it is where you will find the Holy Spirit at work. Indeed, it is the spiritual greenhouse for the Christian life.

The key is what is sometimes called "the means of grace." The word *means* describes a tool or a method. Let's return for a moment to Jacob's 11+ exam.

What are the "means" by which Jacob may pass the 11+? The *effective means* (the power) are his brain and his time spent studying, but the *instrumental means* (the tools) are the workbooks he uses to prepare and the pencil with which he completes the exam.

When it comes to the means of grace, the Holy Spirit is the only effective means. He is the one who unites us to Christ (see 1 Cor. 6:11; 12:12–13) and the one who causes us to grow in Christ (see John 16:12–15; Rom. 8:3–5; Gal. 5:16–25; Eph. 1:17–18; 5:18–20). But the Holy Spirit doesn't do that by zapping us. He uses instrumental means—tools—to help us experience our union with Christ and grow in him.

What are these tools? In the seventeenth century, a group of church ministers called the Westminster Assembly formulated a confession of faith and two catechisms, a set of questions and answers, to help people remember Christian doctrine. Tackling this very question, they wrote, "The outward and ordinary means whereby Christ communicates to us the benefits of redemption are, his ordinances, especially the word, sacraments, and prayer; all of which are made effectual to the elect for salvation."[1] In modern English, the instruments that the Spirit of Christ ordinarily uses to grow Christians are the ministry of the Word, the ministry of the sacraments, and the practice of prayer.

We examined prayer in part 3, and so, in this part, we will focus on the ministry of the Word and the sacraments. We will see that the Holy Spirit is distinct yet inseparable from the means of grace, which means that he is always working through them, albeit in different ways. But before we look at the means themselves, let us examine what the means actually do. They convey grace. As I discussed in chapter 10, the Roman Catholic Church teaches that grace is something conveyed by the sacraments. The Reformers rejected this teaching and insisted that grace is a person—the Lord Jesus Christ. The purpose of the means of grace is to convey *Christ* to believers.

But why is this necessary? Don't we already have Christ? Haven't we already been united to him by faith? The answer, of course, is yes. As we saw in chapter 2, Jesus has undone the great separation. This is all his work, not ours. But it doesn't always feel that way, does it? There are times when we

---

1. Westminster Shorter Catechism, answer 88.

feel incredibly close to God, as if we are basking in his love and presence, and there are other times when we feel cold toward him, as if he is ever so distant from us. What is going on there?

The English puritan John Owen sought to explain this tension by distinguishing between what he called "union" and "communion." Union with Christ is what was achieved by the gospel. We have been united to Christ by faith. Union neither increases nor decreases. We do not become more united or less united to Christ. Union just is—it is fixed and permanent. Communion with God is our *experience* of that union. It is mutual, in the sense that we give and receive; we love, and we are loved. Owen wrote, "Our communion with God consists in his communication of himself to us, with our return to him of that which he requires and accepts, flowing from that union which in Jesus Christ we have with him."[2]

The difference between union and communion is something that all married couples understand and that all those who have observed married couples (namely, everyone) can see. A married couple is united the moment they get married. The officiant pronounces them "husband and wife," and from that moment on, they are united in marriage. Everyone knows, however, that the strength and health of the marriage will depend on how the husband and wife invest in each other—how they commune. A good marriage is built on good communication, loving and being loved, serving and being served, praising and being praised.

In the same way, communion with God is founded on our once-for-all union with Christ. That union is certain and can never be changed, but our experience of it can. Our enjoyment of our relationship with Christ will depend to a large degree on how we pursue him through the means of grace. The purpose of the ministry of the Word and of the sacraments is to present Christ to us, that we may experience and enjoy him. But what does that look like, and how does it happen? We will look at the ministry of the sacraments in chapter 13 and then the ministry of the Word in chapter 14.

---

2. John Owen, *The Works of John Owen*, ed. William H. Goold, vol. 2, *Communion with God* (London: Banner of Truth, 1966), 8–9.

13

THE MINISTRY OF THE SACRAMENTS

> *The sacraments are distinct but inseparable from the realities they signify. They present Christ to us through a physical sign that we may use to receive and enjoy him.*

Our English word *sacrament* comes from the Latin word *sacramentum*, meaning a holy oath or promise. Augustine defined the sacraments as outward and visible signs of inward and invisible grace. They are signs that point away from themselves and toward a greater reality. Just as a road sign is not the destination but points to the destination, so the sacraments are not the reality but point to the reality that is found in Christ.

If you were to guess, what topic do you think occupied the most attention during the debates at the time of the Reformation? From what we saw in the previous part, you might assume that it was the doctrine of justification. It was actually the doctrine of the sacraments. More ink was spilled on this than on any other topic. Why? There were two primary reasons.

First, the Reformers knew that no doctrine stands as an island. What we believe about the sacraments necessarily impacts our understanding of justification by faith, the nature of the church, and the relationship between the Bible and the sacraments.

Second, the Reformers knew that the sacraments were not trivial things. Today, many churches treat baptism and the Lord's Supper as optional extras, which are tagged onto the end of the Sunday service if time allows. The Reformers would have been horrified by such a low view of the sacraments. They were convinced that the sacraments are gifts from the Lord Jesus Christ to his bride, the church. The sacraments matter because they matter to Jesus.

Rome's Errors

There were two aspects of Rome's teaching on the sacraments that particularly troubled the Reformers.

The Doctrine of the Mass

The first concern was the doctrine of the Mass. The Roman Catholic Church understood the Lord's Supper (Holy Communion) to be a re-presentation of Christ's sacrifice. You may have heard of the doctrine of transubstantiation. This is the view that during the celebration of the Lord's Supper, the bread and the wine miraculously turn into the literal body and blood of Jesus. The priest then takes the elements and re-presents them as a sacrifice for sin on the church altar.

This doctrine rips the heart out of Christ's "once for all" sacrifice for sins (see Rom. 6:10; Heb. 10:12–14; 1 Peter 3:18) and makes believers depend on the ongoing work of earthly priests rather than the finished work of the Great High Priest. It robs Christ of glory while transferring power and control to the clergy.

Ex Opere Operato

The second concern relates to how the sacraments operate. The Roman Catholic Church teaches that the sacraments work *ex opere operato*—"from the work worked." This means that they convey grace even if the person who receives them does not come with faith. So Catholics believe that a baby receives grace at baptism even though they are unable to exercise faith and that grace is conveyed through the Lord's Supper even if the recipient does not believe.

The problem is that Rome merges the sign of the sacrament with the reality it signifies, such that receiving the sign is the same as receiving the reality. What, then, is the proper relationship between the sign of the sacrament and the reality it signifies?

Are We Nearly There Yet?

If you're a parent, you'll be familiar with the dreaded cry from the back seat: "Are we nearly there yet?" You'll also be familiar with the answer: not "Shut up!" (unless you're having a really bad day!) but "Look at the sign!" or "Look at the GPS!" Sometimes, the sign tells you that the destination is a long way off; other times, you learn that you're just around the corner. How far away is the sign of the sacraments from the reality they signify?

As we have seen, the Catholic Church teaches that the reality is present *with* the sign. The bread and wine turn into the body and blood of Jesus—they're like big fingers that point down, declaring, "Jesus is here." What about the Reformers, though? You might assume that they came to the opposite view and insisted that the signs are distant from the reality, but their views were actually quite diverse. Some Reformers distinguished the sign and the reality to the point of separation; others so emphasized their inseparability that the sign and the reality became fused. We will look at each of these positions in turn.

Distinct and Separate

On the one side, you have Huldrych (Ulrich) Zwingli, a sixteenth-century minister in Zurich who was also a soldier—in fact, he died on the battlefield in 1531. Zwingli used a military illustration to explain the relationship between the sign and the reality, referencing a great battle that took place at Nähenfels in 1388, after which the Swiss Confederacy was established:

> The word sacrament means a covenant sign or pledge. If a man sews on a white cross, he proclaims that he is a Confederate. And if he makes the pilgrimage to Nähenfels and gives God praise and thanksgiving for the victory vouchsafed to our fathers, he testifies that he is a Confederate indeed. Similarly, the man who receives the mark of baptism is the one who is resolved to hear what God says to him, to learn the divine precepts and to live his life in accordance with them. And the

man who in the remembrance of the Supper gives thanks to God in the congregation testifies to the fact that from the very heart he rejoices in the death of Christ and thanks him for it.[1]

For Zwingli, baptism was like the white cross that the Swiss confederates sewed onto their uniforms to mark their allegiance to the Confederacy, and the Lord's Supper was like the annual pilgrimage that reminded them of their victory. This meant that baptism was a sign that pointed to their own profession of faith, while the Lord's Supper was a sign that pointed to Christ's sacrifice many centuries before. Zwingli separated the reality (Christ) from the sign in both time and space.

Sacraments   Reality

Sacraments as only symbols of the reality

Fig. 13.1. Zwinglian View—Distinct and Separate

Inseparable but Not Distinct

On the other side of the sixteenth-century debate over the sacraments was Martin Luther. He read Jesus's words at the Last Supper, "This is my body" (Mark 14:22), literally and insisted that Jesus's body was physically present every time the church celebrated the Lord's Supper. Like the Roman Catholic Church, Luther taught that the sacraments were a sign of Christ's immediate bodily presence with the church.

The debate became heated—during a meeting at Marburg Castle that was called to resolve the conflict, Luther famously said to Zwingli, "If [Jesus]

---

1. Ulrich Zwingli, "On Baptism," in *Zwingli and Bullinger*, ed. G. W. Bromiley (Philadelphia: Westminster John Knox Press, 1963), 131.

were to order us to eat [excrement] I would do it."² Needless to say, that did not lower the temperature or resolve the dispute.

It is important to note, though, that Luther disagreed with Rome regarding the nature of the Supper and of Christ's presence within it. Like Zwingli and all the other Reformers, Luther utterly opposed the doctrine of the Mass—the idea that Christ's sacrifice is re-presented by the priest. Luther was clear that Christ's sacrifice is once for all.

Luther also rejected the doctrine of transubstantiation—the view that the bread and wine change into the body and blood of Jesus. For Luther, the bread and wine remain what they are but are joined by the body and blood of Jesus, which are physically present "in, with and under" the bread and wine. This view, known as consubstantiation, holds that the reality of the sacraments is physically present with the sign.

Zwingli and Luther were at loggerheads. Luther criticized Zwingli for separating the sign (bread and wine) from the reality (the body and blood of Jesus); Zwingli criticized Luther for fusing the sign and the reality. Zwingli wrote, "If they are the things which they signify they are no longer signs; for sign and thing signified cannot be the same thing."³

Sacraments
Reality

Sacraments are the reality

Fig. 13.2. Lutheran View—Indistinct and Inseparable

Distinct but Inseparable

A few decades later, John Calvin stepped into the debate. He insisted that the sacraments were not "bare" signs that "separate the signs from the

---

2. Michael Mullett, *Martin Luther*, 2nd ed., Routledge Historical Biographies (London: Routledge, 2015), 256.
3. Zwingli, "On Baptism," 131.

realities," because to do so would call into question God's faithfulness.[4] Nor, however, were the sign and the reality the same thing, as both Rome and Luther seemed to suggest. Calvin wrote, "The sacraments of the Lord ought not and cannot at all be separated from their reality and substance. To distinguish them so that they be not confused is not only good and reasonable but wholly necessary. But to divide them so as to set them up the one without the other is absurd. . . . If God cannot deceive or lie, it follows that he performs all that it signifies."[5]

Calvin used the "distinct but inseparable" terminology to describe the relationship between the sacraments and the reality to which they point: Jesus Christ. For Calvin, Jesus is always present and available to be experienced and enjoyed with the sacraments. And yet he remains distinct from them. Jesus is the one who feeds the soul, not the bread and wine, and he does this only for those who come with faith. What does that look like, and in what sense is Christ present with the sacraments?

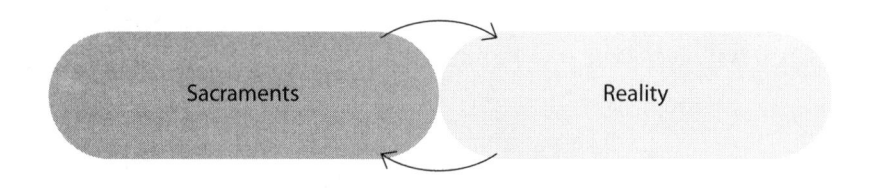

The sacraments cannot be separated from their reality

Fig. 13.3. Calvin's View—Distinct and Inseparable

Highway to Heaven

Both Rome and Luther claimed that Jesus is bodily present at the Lord's Supper. Calvin rejected this for the simple reason that Christ has a fully

---

4. John Calvin, *The First Epistle of Paul the Apostle to the Corinthians*, ed. David W. Torrance and Thomas F. Torrance, trans. William B. Johnston, Calvin's New Testament Commentaries (Grand Rapids: Eerdmans, 1996), 203.
5. John Calvin, "Short Treatise on the Holy Supper of Our Lord and Only Saviour Jesus Christ," in *Calvin: Theological Treatises*, ed. J. K. S. Reid, Library of Christian Classics (Philadelphia: Westminster John Knox Press, 1954), 147–48.

human body, and a human body cannot be in heaven and on earth at the same time. As we saw in chapter 5, our salvation is possible only if Christ assumed a fully human body and soul.[6] According to Calvin, Luther's mistake was to assume that Christ could be present in the Supper only if he was "dragged down" from heaven. He did not understand "the manner of descent by which [Christ] lifts us up to himself."[7]

This is the key. Calvin believed that the Supper provides a highway to heaven. In some mysterious way, when we celebrate the Lord's Supper, the Holy Spirit lifts our souls to heaven, and we experience our union with Christ. Calvin admitted that this teaching is mysterious and that it was something he must "rather experience than understand," but he insisted that it was biblical.[8]

The most important text in support of Calvin's view is 1 Corinthians 10:16. Paul warns his readers about the danger of idolatry, and then he asks, "Is not the cup of thanksgiving for which we give thanks a participation in the blood of Christ? And is not the bread that we break a participation in the body of Christ?" Paul's point is that it is utterly incongruous to live for idols in one moment and then for Christ in the next, but he says this in a most striking way. He describes the Lord's Supper as a "participation" in the body and blood of Christ.

A number of Bible commentators explain this verse away by pointing out that the "body of Christ" refers to the church in the next verse (v. 17)—therefore, they argue, verse 16 likely refers to the church as well. The problem is that no other passage of the Bible describes the church as the "blood of Christ." Indeed, it would appear to be a thoroughly inappropriate metaphor for the church. A more convincing interpretation of this passage is that it describes a spiritual form of participation in Christ that we experience

---

6. Gregory of Nazianzus wrote, "What has not been assumed has not been healed." Gregory of Nazianzus, Letter 101, in *The Christian Theology Reader*, ed. Alister E. McGrath, 3rd ed. (Oxford: Blackwell Publishing, 2007), 270. Since human bodies cannot be in more than one place at one time, it is impossible for Christ's body to be physically present wherever and whenever the Lord's Supper is celebrated. If it were, it would be a phantom body that is unable to save. See Calvin, *Institutes of the Christian Religion*, ed. John T. McNeill, trans. Ford Lewis Battles (Philadelphia: Westminster John Knox Press, 1960), 4.17.16, 29; Calvin, "Short Treatise on the Holy Supper of Our Lord and Only Saviour Jesus Christ," 158.

7. John Calvin, *Institutes*, 4.17.16.

8. Calvin, 4.17.32.

when we celebrate the Lord's Supper together.[9] By the power of the Spirit, who is able "to join together things separated by a great distance," we are spiritually lifted up to heaven to enjoy Christ.[10]

Let us review the different understandings of the sacraments.

For Zwingli, the sign of the sacraments was not only distinguished from the reality they signified but also separated from it. The sacraments are mere visual aids that help us to remember Christ as we await his return. This view is dominant in the evangelical church today, which perhaps explains why the sacraments are treated so lightly and trivially.

Luther and Rome recognized that the sign and the reality are inseparable but failed to distinguish between them, viewing the Supper as a crude consumption of Christ's physical body and blood. This is implausible, and it does great damage to our understanding of the humanity of Christ.

Calvin's view, by contrast, was thoroughly biblical and far more glorious. He showed how the sacraments are the place where Christ is presented to us, that we may experience, enjoy, feed on, and delight in him.

An analogy may help. My wife and I recently went to the Yorkshire Dales for a couple of nights to celebrate our anniversary. The Dales are beautiful—rolling hills, gorgeous rivers, a pub on every corner—but the best thing was that Anna and I got to spend time together. We did the things we normally do at home—walk, talk, eat—but those two days away were worth more than two months of ordinary life.

Why? Because that's where we communed, away from the distractions of work, raising children, and ministering in a busy church. We were able to enjoy each other, delight in each other, love each other. It deepened our experience of the union we have in marriage. We felt closer to each other.

That is exactly what we receive in the sacraments. They enable us to experience a deeper communion with Christ. In baptism and the Lord's Supper, we get to feel in our body the experience of being washed, fed, nourished, sustained, loved, and cherished by Christ. The sacraments are a foretaste and an anticipation of that glorious day when we will be face-to-face with Jesus

---

9. For a fuller defense of Calvin's doctrine of the Lord's Supper, see Ralph Cunnington, "Calvin's Doctrine of the Lord's Supper: A blot upon his labors as a public instructor?" *Westminster Theological Journal* 73, no. 2 (Fall 2011): 220. Available at https://www.academia.edu/1091130/Calvins_Doctrine_of_the_Lords_Supper_A_blot_upon_his_labors_as_a_public_instructor.

10. Calvin, *The First Epistle of Paul the Apostle to the Corinthians*, 247.

himself. As Calvin wrote, they are a place where we "may grow more and more together with him, until he perfectly joins us with him in the heavenly life."[11] They are the spiritual greenhouse for the Christian life.

Living It Out: Hunger for the Sacraments

If all this is true, then we should hunger for the sacraments and enjoy them as much as we can. But let me be direct with you: if we come from a low-church evangelical tradition, we are unlikely to think this way. We are far more likely to think, "I get Christ when I read the Bible and listen to sermons. Why do I need the sacraments?"

It is true that baptism and the Lord's Supper do not give us anything that we can't receive from the Word of God. Just like the Word, they present Christ to us to be received and enjoyed. But they present him in a different manner. Have you ever tried to explain what snow is to someone who has never seen snow before? It's difficult: "Well, it's this soft, cold, white stuff that melts in your hand." But if you show them a pile of snow, they'll understand right away; they will be able to see and feel it.

The Word presents Christ and his promises in an audible form. The sacraments present him visually and kinesthetically—you can see, touch, and feel them. No one has expressed it better than Robert Bruce in his sixteenth-century sermons on the Lord's Supper:

> Even if you get the same thing [in the sacrament] which you get in the Word, yet you get that same thing better. What is this "better"? . . . We get a better grip of Christ now, for by the Sacrament my faith is nourished, the bounds of my soul are enlarged, and so where I had but a little grip of Christ before, as it were, between my finger and my thumb, now I get him in my whole hand, and indeed the more my faith grows, the better grip I get of Christ Jesus. Thus the Sacrament is very necessary, if only for the reason that we get Christ better, and get a firmer grasp of him by the Sacrament than we could have before.[12]

---

11. Calvin, *Institutes*, 4.17.33.
12. Robert Bruce, *The Mystery of the Lord's Supper*, trans. Thomas Torrance (Fearn, UK: Christian Focus Publications, 2005), 84–85.

Making It Personal

1. Have you ever heard the Christian life described in terms of union and communion? Does that distinction help you understand some of the struggles you have or have had in your faith? Explain.
2. Think about the times in which you've felt closest to God—after reading this chapter, do you think that sense of closeness was related to regular communion with him?
3. How has thinking through the role of the Lord's Supper helped you understand its importance? Do you tend to think of this sacrament as a mere memory aid of Christ's death on the cross or as a participation with Christ? Why do you think that is?
4. How will this chapter help you approach the table with more anticipation and excitement the next time your church shares the Lord's Supper? What will you do to better prepare yourself for it?

14

THE MINISTRY OF THE WORD

> *The Word written is distinct but inseparable from the Holy Spirit. This means that we should approach God's Word—both as we study it and as we hear it preached—with prayer and with the expectation that we will meet Christ in it.*

A children's Sunday school teacher was starting a new series on famous missionaries throughout church history. She held up a photograph of Jim Elliot, an American missionary to the Huaorani people of Ecuador, and asked if anyone knew who he was. The children looked puzzled and scratched their heads. Eventually, a brave eight-year-old tentatively raised his hand and asked, "Miss, is it Jesus?"

Nine times out of ten, either "Jesus" or "Read the Bible more often" will be the right answer in Sunday school class—and for good reason. Jesus himself showed that the entire Bible points to him (Luke 24:27), and the Bible claims to be powerful. It is "living and active," Hebrews 4:12 tells us, and "sharper than any two-edged sword" (ESV). The prophet Isaiah insisted that God's Word always accomplishes his purposes: "As the rain and the snow come down from heaven, and do not return to it without watering the earth . . . so is my word that goes out from my mouth: It will not return to me empty, but will accomplish what I desire and achieve the purpose for which I sent it" (Isa. 55:10–11). Indeed, the Bible is how God equips and grows his people:

> All Scripture is God-breathed and is useful for teaching, rebuking, correcting and training in righteousness, so that the servant of God may be thoroughly equipped for every good work. (2 Tim. 3:16–17)

If we want to grow as Christians, if we want to be fully equipped to live for Christ and his glory, then we need to depend on the Word of God. Like the sacraments, the Bible is the spiritual greenhouse for the Christian life. But isn't there more to it than that? Surely the Holy Spirit is at work in other ways today. And if he is, don't we need to follow his work wherever it may be found?

What Type of Church Are You?

In September, new arrivals flock to Manchester. Some are attending one of the five universities in the city. Others are starting new jobs. It's a time when lots of people check out City Church, and they often ask me, "What type of church are you?" They are usually asking about our worship style, sermon length, or approach to spiritual gifts.

Every now and then I'm asked, "Are you a Word church or a Spirit church?" When I hear that question, I just want to tear my hair out. It's a bit like asking, "Are you a human with a brain or a human with lungs?" or "Is it a car with a steering wheel or a car with wheels?" God's Word and the Holy Spirit are central to the life of every church. A congregation that lacks either the Word or the Spirit could not be a true church. Indeed, the Word is completely dependent on and inseparable from the Holy Spirit.

Inspiration of the Bible

It was the Holy Spirit who gave us the Bible. As we've seen, Paul describes the Scriptures as "God-breathed" (2 Tim. 3:16). The Greek word he uses contains the root of the word for Spirit (*pneuma*). God breathed out the words of Scripture through the Holy Spirit.

Peter explains how this happened in his second letter. He tells his readers that "no prophecy of Scripture came about by the prophet's own interpretation of things" (1:20). Instead, the "prophets, though human, spoke from God as they were carried along by the Holy Spirit" (v. 21). The Holy Spirit is the primary author of the Bible. He spoke through the mouths of the authors, and he wrote through their pens.

Proclamation of the Bible

The Holy Spirit equips people to teach the Bible. In Acts 6, the members of the Synagogue of the Freedmen strongly opposed Stephen as he preached the gospel in Jerusalem. He kept going, however, and we read that "they could not stand up against the wisdom the Spirit gave him as he spoke" (v. 10). In a similar vein, Paul insisted that his message and his preaching were "not with wise and persuasive words, but with a demonstration of the Spirit's power" (1 Cor. 2:4).

Illumination of the Bible

The Holy Spirit is the one who enables people to understand the Scriptures. When Paul and Silas arrived in Philippi, they found no church in the city. Indeed, it appears that there was not even a synagogue there, so on the Sabbath day, they left to look for a place of prayer. Outside the city, they found a group of women gathered by a river to worship God. One of them was named Lydia, a wealthy woman from nearby Thyatira, who had made her fortune selling purple cloth. Paul began to preach the Word to the women, and "the Lord opened [Lydia's] heart to respond to Paul's message" (Acts 16:14). Without the Holy Spirit, it is impossible to understand the Bible in a way that leads to salvation and Christian growth.

The Holy Spirit and the written Word (the Scriptures) are inseparably linked.[1] The written Word depends on the Holy Spirit for its creation, proclamation, and reception, while the Holy Spirit depends on the Word to be his instrument in the world. The universe was created by the Word (see Gen. 1:3), the dead are raised by the Word (see Mark 5:41–42; John 11:41–44), spiritual life is given by the Word (see Ezek. 37:1–14; James 1:18; 1 Peter 1:23), and the church is washed by the Word (see Eph. 5:26).

---

1. In John 1:1, God the Son is described as the Word who was with God in the beginning. Scripture distinguishes between the Word written (the Scriptures) and the Word incarnate (Jesus). Throughout this chapter, I am only referring to the former when I speak of the Word.

The relationship between the Word and the Spirit could not be closer, but Christians don't always recognize this.

The Word and the Spirit

The different positions Christians hold regarding the relationship between the Word and the Spirit can be neatly summarized using the "distinct but inseparable" formula.

Distinct and Separate

Some Christians teach that the Word and the Spirit are not only distinct but also separate. There are two versions of this teaching: the charismatic version and the conservative version.

The charismatic version is the one that asks, "What sort of church are you?" Churches in this tradition insist on a rigid separation between the ministry of the Word and the ministry of the Spirit in their services. The sermon is where Word ministry takes place, as the preacher opens up the Bible and fills people's hearts and minds with knowledge about God. This is followed by a "ministry time," where the Spirit is welcomed into the service. Through music and the use of spiritual gifts, the congregation doesn't merely learn more about God—they also experience him in profound and life-changing ways. The charismatic version of separation sees these "ministry times" as the spiritual greenhouse of the Christian life.

The conservative version is quite different. It does not have separate times for Word and Spirit ministry but insists that the spiritual power for salvation and Christian growth is to be found in the Spirit himself, not in the Bible (see Acts 16:14). Since the Holy Spirit "blows wherever [he] pleases" (John 3:8), he sometimes accompanies the preaching of the Word and sometimes does not. This is known as "unction"—the Holy Spirit sometimes anoints the preached Word but sometimes does not.

On July 8, 1741, Jonathan Edwards preached his famous sermon "Sinners in the Hands of an Angry God" at a church in Enfield, Connecticut. The response was phenomenal, as people interrupted him mid-sermon to ask how they may be saved. Edwards had preached the sermon before, and he preached it many times after, but he saw very little outward response from his listeners. Why the difference? The answer, according to the conservative separation view, is that the Spirit anointed and accompanied Edwards's preaching at Enfield but did not do so elsewhere.[2]

Word   Spirit

**The Spirit can work without the Word,
and the Word can be preached without the Spirit**

Fig. 14.1. "The Spirit Has Not Turned Up" View—Distinct and Separate

Inseparable but Not Distinct

Though some separate the Word and the Spirit, others so emphasize their inseparability that they fail to acknowledge a distinction between them. "Let the Word do the work," they say, emphasizing the importance of "Word ministry" in the expectation that, wherever the Bible is preached, fruit will necessarily grow.[3] This approach has the merit of recognizing that God works through his Word, but it adopts an almost mechanical view of the relationship between the Word and the Spirit in which they are merged and intermingled.

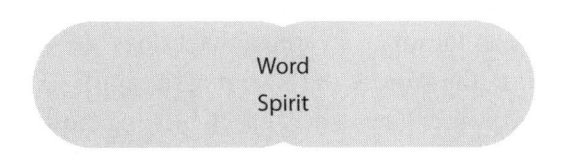

Word
Spirit

Where there is preaching, there is the Spirit

Fig. 14.2. "The Word Will Do the Work" View—Indistinct and Inseparable

2. See, for example, Robert Strivens, "Preaching—'Ex Opere Operato?,'" in *The Truth Shall Make You Free*, ed. Roger Fay (Stoke, UK: Tentmaker Publications, 2008), 57.
3. See, for example, the title of a recent collection of essays: Peter Bolt, ed., *Let the Word Do the Work: Essays in Honour of Phillip D. Jensen* (Sydney: Matthias Media, 2015).

Distinct but Inseparable

There is a third approach to the relationship between the Word and the Spirit, and that is to recognize that they are distinct yet inseparable. The Word performs the same function as the sacraments. As John Calvin wrote, they both "offer and set forth Christ to us, and in him the treasure of heavenly grace."[4] Wherever and whenever the Word of God is preached and shared, the Holy Spirit makes Christ present. They are inseparable, but they remain distinct in the function they perform as they present Christ.

At the beginning of this part, I used my son's 11+ test to illustrate how the means of grace work. Jacob's brain and his diligence are the effective means of passing the test—they provide the power—but his workbook and his pencil are the instrumental means. In the ministry of the Word, the Holy Spirit is the effective means of presenting Christ to us, and the Word is the instrumental means he uses. This is exactly what the apostles taught when they wrote that God "chose to give us birth through the word of truth" (James 1:18) and enabled us to be "born again . . . through the living and enduring word of God" (1 Peter 1:23).

If Christ is present whenever the Word is preached, and if the Spirit is inseparably connected to the Word, how do we explain why the Word impacts people differently? Here we come to another aspect of what it means for the Spirit to be distinct from the Word. The Spirit always accompanies the Word—but not always to the same effect. The apostle Paul described ministers of the Word as the "aroma of Christ among those who are being saved and those who are perishing. To the one we [ministers] are an aroma that brings death; to the other, an aroma that brings life" (2 Cor. 2:15–16).

In other words, the Word is the "sword of the Spirit" (Eph. 6:17), but it is a double-edged sword. It has a dual effect, blessing those who come with faith and judging those who don't. This is unsurprising, given that the Word presents Christ—indeed, Christ himself said that he came with a sword to turn "a man against his father, a daughter against her mother" (Matt. 10:35).

The Word divides people because the Spirit accompanies it with distinct and different purposes. For believers, the Holy Spirit makes the Word a

---

4. John Calvin, *Institutes of the Christian Religion*, ed. John T. McNeill, trans. Ford Lewis Battles (Philadelphia: Westminster John Knox Press, 1960), 4.14.17.

"perennial fountain that will never fail us."[5] For unbelievers, the Holy Spirit accompanies the Word in judgment as long as they continue in their unbelief.[6]

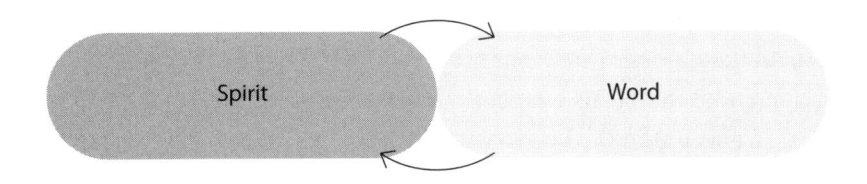

The Spirit works in different ways through the preached Word

Fig. 14.3. Calvin's View—Distinct and Inseparable

Living It Out: Communing through the Word and the Spirit

Let the Word Dwell in You Richly

If the Word of God is a "perennial fountain that will never fail us," we must run to it, expecting the Word to refresh, delight, and shape our hearts and minds.

What will that mean? It will mean that we are committed to expository preaching—preaching that lets the main message of the Bible's text be the main message of the sermon. This is because we know that the Bible, rather than a preacher's flair or skill, is God's chosen means of blessing his people. We will also expect our spiritual thirst to be satisfied by every part of the Bible. The Spirit doesn't just accompany the reading and preaching of John 3:16; he is present to bless the lists in 1 Chronicles, the genealogy in Genesis 5, and the spectacular apocalyptic scenes in Revelation 20. Wherever we turn in the Bible, we expect the Spirit to bless us when we come with faith.

---

5. John Calvin, *The Gospel According to John, Part 1*, ed. David W. Torrance and Thomas F. Torrance, trans. T. H. L. Parker (Grand Rapids: Eerdmans, 1959), 93.

6. John Calvin wrote, "The Spirit convicts men in the preaching of the Gospel in two ways. Some are touched seriously and humble themselves of their own accord and assent willingly to the judgment which condemns them. Others, although they are convinced of guilt and cannot escape, do not yield in sincerity or submit themselves to the authority and control of the Holy Spirit." See John Calvin, *The Gospel According to John, Part 2*, ed. David W. Torrance and Thomas F. Torrance, trans. T. H. L. Parker (Grand Rapids: Eerdmans, 1961), 116.

We also expect the Spirit to bless us regardless of a preacher's oratorical gifts. When a preacher steps up to the lectern and begins his sermon with a droning, monotone quote from a seventeenth-century Puritan commentary, we may be tempted to switch off our minds and assume that we will get nothing out of the sermon. That is our problem, not the Word's. The preacher may be poor, and if that is his own fault due to laziness or neglect, he will have to give an account to the Lord for it (see Heb. 13:17). But if he is preaching the Word, the Spirit *will* accompany the preaching for our blessing, and it is our responsibility to receive the Word with faith.

This means that we will approach the Word with both expectancy and prayer: expectancy because we know that God has promised to work through his Word, and prayer because we depend on the Spirit's gracious provision.

If we think that the Spirit accompanies the Word only occasionally (the distinct and separate view), we will pray like crazy but will have low expectations for what God will do, because we don't know whether the Spirit is going to turn up or not.

If we think that the Spirit automatically yields fruit whenever the Word is opened (the inseparable but not distinct view), we will work hard on our study but will hardly take the time to pray, because we will assume that all we need to do is study the Word.

Only if we grasp that the Spirit accompanies the Word distinctly yet inseparably will we pray expectantly. Then, we will know that the Spirit blesses those who come to the Word with faith as expressed through prayer.

Finally, if the Spirit has pledged to accompany the Word, we should expect him to do so in a variety of forms and settings, not simply in preaching and in small-group Bible studies. Writing to the church in Colossae, Paul exhorted the saints to "let the word of Christ dwell in you richly, teaching and admonishing one another in all wisdom, singing psalms and hymns and spiritual songs, with thankfulness in your hearts to God." (Col. 3:16 ESV).

The charismatic version of the "distinct and separate" view teaches that the Spirit turns up only after the sermon, when the band leads a "ministry time." As we have seen, that view is flawed—the Spirit does accompany the preached Word. But it is also true that the Spirit accompanies sung worship. Notice that when Paul exhorts the Colossians to let the word of

Christ dwell in them richly, he tells them to do so by singing the Word to one another.

Sung worship, rightly understood, *is* Word ministry, and it has a peculiar power to penetrate our hearts with the Word. Theologian John Frame explains, "Poetic-musical forms impart vividness and memorability to God's words. That vividness and memorability, in turn, drive the word into our hearts, so that it becomes precious to us and motivates us to praise and obedience. . . . God is not interested only in getting his word into our hands; he wants to get it into our hearts (Pss. 1; 119:11, 24, 36, 69, etc.; Col. 3:16)."[7] We should approach sung worship with care—insisting that we sing songs that are saturated in God's Word—but also with prayer and with the expectation that the Spirit will be present to bless us through it.

It is worth noting that this both permits and requires flexibility in forms and styles of sung worship. The content of our songs presents Christ to us, and the musical elements aid both our memory and our affectionate engagement with him. If we always insist on musical forms and styles that suit our ethnic and cultural background, we benefit ourselves but fail to serve those in our churches who come from different backgrounds. This is not to say that our musical style should be constantly changing, but it is to say that we should be mindful of these matters as we seek to pursue unity in diversity within our churches.

Commit to Communion

As we close part 5, we need to hear one message loud and clear: we must commit to communion with Christ. The Word and the sacraments are the very means by which we enjoy our union with Christ and grow up as Christians. But sometimes it's a slog. There are times in our lives when we feel spiritually dry, when merely opening the Bible feels like a marathon effort, when we cannot remember a single point from an entire sermon series on the book of Romans. It feels so depressing. What is wrong with us?

We know that the Lord's Supper is a precious gift from Jesus—something we should hunger after and delight in. Yet sometimes when we hear the words of institution, we just wish that it was over already so that we could

---

7. John M. Frame, *Worship in Spirit and Truth* (Phillipsburg, NJ: P&R, 1996), 112–13.

go home and put the chicken in the oven. What's going on? Communing on this side of Christ's return is hard work. There are no silver bullets because we are sinners living in a broken world.

When a couple comes in for marriage counseling, I usually know fairly quickly where the problems lie. There are certain tell-tale signs that reveal why the marriage is in trouble. Sometimes the problem is a third party. The husband has developed a crush on a colleague at work. He hasn't acted on it yet, but it's always there, lurking in the back of his mind, suffocating his relationship with his wife. Similarly, we may find communion with Christ through his Word and the sacraments so difficult because something or someone else has captured our hearts, strangling our enjoyment of our union with Christ.

In other marriages, the problem isn't attraction to a third party, but simply neglect. The wife has started to take her husband for granted. Their relationship has become entirely functional. They are more like housemates than soulmates, and they fail to spend quality time together. Likewise, our communion with Christ might be a slog because we are neglecting it. We do our quiet times, but we schedule them for the five-minute time slot before we head off to work in the morning. We listen to sermons, but we check our emails at the same time, like the husband who talks with his wife while checking the football scores.

In still other marriages, the problem is a circumstance—financial difficulties, the loss of a job, a death in the family—and the couple is left struggling to communicate well about it. One spouse has not lived up to the other's expectations, or they feel misunderstood. In the same way, we may struggle to commune with God because of difficult circumstances. We struggle to understand why God has allowed these things to happen, and we are secretly angry with him. We wouldn't say it out loud, but we know that we harbor bitterness in our hearts. This makes us reluctant to spend time with God, poisoning our thoughts against him.

No marriage has ever been saved by the couple spending less time together. The only remedy is communion—talking together, spending time together, seeking to understand each other. Communion, through good times and bad, is what grows a relationship.

Our earthly spouse will let us down. Our heavenly spouse never will. But this does not mean that the relationship will be easy. Every relationship requires hard work, and if we want to grow up in Christ, we need to commit ourselves to delighting in him through the Word and the sacraments. We must hunger for sound expository preaching, prioritize personal devotions, and prepare ourselves for the sacraments through prayer and focused reflection, that we may "get Christ better" in them.[8] Such communion will draw us closer to Christ, aligning our hearts with his and causing them to overflow with joy and thankfulness.

Making It Personal

1. How would you summarize a biblical view of preaching?
2. How could understanding the distinct but inseparable nature of the Word and the Spirit in preaching help you engage more deeply with next Sunday's sermon?
3. Take a few minutes to reflect on how the Spirit has used preaching to convict you of sin, encourage you to love him more, and help you live for Christ. Make a list, and then thank God for using those who have faithfully taught the Word to build you up.
4. If you're feeling distant from God at the moment, which of the marital analogies do you think best describes your struggles?
5. How could you better prioritize the spiritual resources that God has given to his people to help address these issues? How could you encourage others in your church to do the same?

Further Reading for Part 5

Cunnington, Ralph. *Preaching with Spiritual Power: Calvin's Understanding of Word and Spirit in Preaching*. Fearn, UK: Christian Focus Publications, 2015.

Ferguson, Sinclair B. *The Holy Spirit*. Contours of Christian Theology. Leicester: IVP Academic, 1996.

Frame, John M. *Worship in Spirit and Truth*. Phillipsburg, NJ: P&R Publishing, 1996.

Letham, Robert. *The Lord's Supper: Eternal Word in Broken Bread*. Phillipsburg, NJ: P&R Publishing, 2012.

---

8. See the quote from Robert Bruce at the end of chapter 13.

Part 6

What Is the Church?

My friend Nick took one of his classmates to a Balti curry restaurant in the student district of Birmingham. As they took their seats, they noticed some students at another table laughing uncontrollably and having a marvelous time. After a while, Nick's friend pointed to the table and said, "I bet those people are Christians." Nick was startled. His friend was not a Christian, and Nick knew that he was pretty skeptical about Christianity. Why did he think those students were Christians? Surely it wasn't because they were laughing and having fun!

But when Nick looked at the table, he actually recognized them: they were all students from the Christian Union. How did his friend know? When Nick asked, he replied, "You see that guy there—the one with rippling muscles—well, he's a member of the university rugby team. And see, he's sitting next to that geeky looking girl from my computer science class. There's someone from India, someone from China, and I'm sure I can hear French and Spanish accents too. There's no way a group that diverse would be hanging out together—not unless they were Christians!"

Nick's friend wasn't yet a Christian, but he had wonderfully grasped something of what the gospel can do: it can unite diverse people as one.

In chapter 2, we saw how the rejection of the distinction between humanity and God brought about a terrible separation. Adam and Eve wanted to be like God (sin), and that led to separation (death): they were immediately separated from God, and, over time, they were separated from each other as sin polluted and distorted every aspect of their lives and every relationship that they had.

In the last part of this book, we are going to examine how the gospel repairs those broken relationships and forms one new, diverse people—the church. We're going to examine this in three different spheres of diversity: gifting, gender, and ethnicity.

15

ONE CHURCH WITH MANY GIFTS

Before I was a pastor, I taught law at a university. My colleagues and I welcomed over 250 new students each year. Of those 250 students, less than a quarter would go on to practice law. Why would they spend so much time and money studying law, when they knew that there were not enough jobs for all of them at the end of their studies? One of the reasons, I think, is because they wanted the status that comes from having studied law at a British university.

Twenty-first-century Anglo-Americans tend to think that people are what they do. When we meet someone new, we usually begin the conversation by asking two questions: (1) What's your name? and (2) What do you do? Those two questions help us to ascertain a person's identity.

In our culture, we derive identity from doing. We find dignity in function. What's more, we have imported this way of thinking into the church. Lots of young men in the church desire to be preachers and leaders. If you are looking for someone to teach a seminar series in your Sunday school track, it is usually easy to find volunteers. Finding someone to lead your hospitality, cleaning, or mercy ministry teams is much harder. Why?

I think it is because we seek to derive our identity from what we do, and, consciously or subconsciously, we develop a hierarchy of church roles in our heads. This means that we all end up wanting to do the same things—the more important roles (at least as we perceive them). We derive our identity from our church role and find affinity with those who do the same thing. This means that we pursue unity through a homogeneity of gifting. But that is not the way God has designed the church to function.

The New Testament uses a number of different metaphors to describe the church: a family, a body, a bride, a building, and a business. Quite often, we privilege the metaphor we find most appealing in order to reinforce our own particular perspective on the church.

The metaphor of choice in more recent times has been the church as a *family*. This is an important metaphor that has ample biblical precedent (see Gal. 6:10; Eph. 2:19; 1 Tim. 5:1–2). It is also radically appealing to a society fragmented by family breakdown, one in which people are yearning for a meaningful community. If, however, we privilege the family metaphor at the expense of other biblical metaphors, we are liable to end up with a distorted perception of the church.

In particular, such a perception may lead us to adopt a consumerist mindset whereby we look to the church merely as a means to provide the relationships, care, and community that we crave. This makes church about us rather than about Jesus, and it will mean that our commitment to church will be tied to what it gives us rather than how we can serve others. Ultimately, it will mean that we leave a church whenever it does not meet our felt needs. The metaphor of the church as a family must be balanced by the metaphor of the church as a body.

A Spiritual Way to View Aptitudes

In several places, the New Testament describes the church as a body and uses this metaphor to teach a number of different truths. Ephesians 5:23 teaches that Christ is the head of his body, the church. The emphasis in 1 Corinthians 12, however, is that the church is *one* body with *many* diverse and complementary parts.

It is important to understand the context of 1 Corinthians 12. Paul is writing to the church in Corinth—a city awash with idols and pagan worship. He has been systematically working through a list of issues in the life of the church, and, from chapter 10 onward, Paul has been addressing the subject of worship in the church. He seeks to show how completely different Christian worship should be from pagan worship. In 1 Corinthians 12, he begins to address the topic of spiritual gifts.

Now, the word rendered as "spiritual gifts" in some of our English translations (such as the ESV) is found for the first time in verse 1, but the original Greek uses a different word, which literally means "spiritual things." Paul is making a subtle but important point here. He wants the Corinthians to see the contrast between how they used to think about gifts when they were pagans (see v. 2) and how they ought to think about gifts now that they are Christians—"spiritual" people (v. 1).

You see, the pagan way of thinking is to view gifts as things that belong to us: we have acquired our "talents," "aptitudes," and "competencies" through our own hard work and determination. This understanding leads us to see gifts as our own personal attributes, which give us respect and status and which we use to feed our dominant idol—ourselves.

The apostle Paul wants both the Corinthians and the church at large to see things very differently. Everything we have, even our natural abilities (like strength, flair, or an eye for a good deal), is a gift. These gifts are undeserved and have been given to us by God to be used in the service of others. This radically changes how we view all our competencies, but Paul has a particular type of gift in mind here. He describes it as *charismata*, a Greek word meaning grace. These "grace gifts" are supernatural abilities that God the Holy Spirit distributes (see v. 4) and that, when used, are manifestations of the Holy Spirit through us. And the incredible thing is that they have been given to every single Christian (see v. 7).

One God Gives Many Gifts

Every single Christian has been given a spiritual gift, and each gift is different. That is the message of verses 4–6:

> There are *different* kinds of gifts, but the *same* Spirit distributes them. There are *different* kinds of service, but the *same* Lord. There are *different* kinds of working, but in all of them and in everyone it is the *same* God at work.

The God who is "one" (v. 9) and "the same" (v. 4) gives a vast array of gifts to his people. Paul lists some of those diverse gifts in verses 8–11, but this is only meant to be a snapshot, not an exhaustive catalog. We know that because there is another list of spiritual gifts in verses 28–30, as well as three further lists in Romans 12:6–8, Ephesians 4:11, and 1 Peter 4:11.

Theologians disagree about how many gifts there are in total because there is some overlap between the lists, but it seems clear that none of the lists are intended to be exhaustive. They are simply indicative—the point is that there is an incredible diversity of gifts that the Lord gives to his church.

Some of the gifts are Word-ministry gifts, such as teaching (see 12:28), prophecy (see 12:28), and "message[s] of knowledge" (12:8). Others are gifts that facilitate worship, such as the gift of tongues and the gift of interpretation (see 12:10).[1] The gifts of healing and helping (see 12:28) are for practical service in areas of mercy ministry. And the gift of "guidance" (12:28), or administration, is given to help devise strategies and implement structures for the ministry of the church. It is the gift of "strategic statesmanship."[2] The gift of "faith" (12:9) does not refer to the gift of saving faith, which is given to all believers. Rather, it describes the gift of being able to discern opportunities and then lead others in taking calculated risks for the sake of the gospel and the advancement of the kingdom. It is the gift of vision, which believes in the God of the impossible and then prays, plans, and leads others in faith.

In an age of genetic testing, it might seem surprising that law enforcement still uses fingerprinting to identify suspects rather than relying on DNA evidence. The reason is because the fingerprints of identical twins will usually differ, while their DNA will be the same. When a baby is developing in the womb, the outer skin around their fingers will grow first. Only later on in the pregnancy will an additional layer of skin begin to develop beneath the outer skin—this layer will develop more quickly, giving rise to the folds and ridges that make up the fingerprints. Fingerprints are developmental rather than genetic, making them unique.

---

1. Some Christians believe that certain gifts were only for the apostolic era (cessationism), while others believe that all gifts remain in use today (continuationism). Compare Sinclair B. Ferguson, *The Holy Spirit*, Contours of Christian Theology (Leicester: IVP Academic, 1996) and D. A. Carson, *Showing the Spirit: A Theological Exposition of 1 Corinthians 12-14* (Grand Rapids: Baker, 1987).

2. Anthony C. Thiselton, *The First Epistle to the Corinthians*, The New International Greek Testament Commentary (Carlisle, UK: Paternoster Press, 2000), 1022.

Spiritual gifts are similar. The one God has given the one church a diverse range of gifts. The Holy Spirit gifts each believer, and, as these gifts develop, they become unique to the individual believer.

This is so important to understand. Inevitably, Christians have their heroes of the faith whom they admire and seek to emulate. For some, these are the theological heavyweights of the past, like John Calvin, or the influential pastors of the present, like Kevin DeYoung; for others, they are senior saints who model a quiet life of prayer, service, and faithfulness.

It is good to follow godly examples—in fact, the apostle Paul encourages us to do this just one chapter earlier: "Follow my example, as I follow the example of Christ" (1 Cor. 11:1). We must be careful, however, not to rigidly imitate other believers. Nor should we be discouraged if we think we are less gifted than others. The one Spirit has gifted each of us differently, and he has allowed those gifts to be distinctively shaped by our own character and life experiences.

In stark contrast, our culture encourages us to ape others. The mighty advertising industry depends on our desire to be like celebrities in order to sell its products. We need to resist this homogenizing pressure and celebrate that God has made each of us distinctive. Moreover, he has gifted every single believer with gifts that are unique to them, and he has commanded us to use those gifts for the common good of the church in which he has placed us.

One Body, Many Parts

As I noted above, Paul uses the image of a body to describe this mutual dependence within the church. Paul writes of this image, "Just as a body, though one, has many parts, but all its many parts form one body, so it is with Christ" (1 Cor. 12:12). The church is one body made up of many parts, and the parts need one another. We should not assume, simply because we are unlike other people, that we do not fit in the church (see vv. 15–16). Nor should we tell others who are different from us that they do not belong in the church (see v. 21).

In Corinth, it seems that the gift of tongues was valued above all others (see 1 Cor. 14:18–19). That is still the case in certain parts of the charismatic and Pentecostal church today. More conservative churches run the risk of elevating Word-ministry gifts above all others and devaluing the gifts of administration, helping, and faith.

The illustration of a human body helps here. The body would be horribly disfigured if it were just made up of hundreds of eyes (see v. 17). Its beauty and functionality depend on the diversity of its parts. Moreover, each part depends on the others. The eye would be helpless to act on what it sees if the body did not have hands to respond. The head could do very little if the body did not have feet and legs to carry it (see v. 21). The parts of the body —and, by implication, the members of the church—*need* one another. We need one another, in all of our glorious diversity, to fulfill our collective and individual purpose of glorifying God and enjoying him forever.[3]

For that reason, while we remain distinct from one another in gifting, we are also very much inseparable from one another in purpose. This is precisely the point that Paul makes in verses 22 to 27. The stronger and more prominent parts of the body need to look after the weaker and less presentable parts, because they depend on those parts for life and vitality. The parts are inseparable: "If one part suffers, every part suffers with it; if one part is honored, every part rejoices with it" (v. 26).

The same is true of the church. We are distinct from one another in our gifting, character, temperament, and life experience. But we are inseparable from one another in our common goal of glorifying God and in our life together, to use Dietrich Bonhoeffer's phrase.[4] We need one another for health, life, and vitality. When one of us suffers, we all suffer; when one succeeds, we all succeed. Jesus issued his Great Commission to the church, in all its glorious and inseparable diversity.

Living It Out: Value and Cultivate the Church's Distinctive Gifts

We need to value and cultivate the distinctive gifts that God has given each of us. So, if you're an introvert who loves poring over budget sheets,

---

3. See Westminster Shorter Catechism, question and answer 1.
4. Dietrich Bonhoeffer, *Life Together* (New York: HarperOne, 1978).

that's not a character flaw. It's not something about which you need to be embarrassed, nor is it a quality you need to hide or change. No, it is how God has distinctively gifted and shaped you to serve "the common good" (1 Cor. 12:7).

If you are a dreamer, the sort of person who has grand visions about what could be, if you are unafraid to step out in faith with great expectations about what God might do, don't see that as a problem, even if it frustrates those around you. Steward this gift well—learn patience, and see how God will use your gift of faith for the common good.

Perhaps you are the sort of person who sees Bible study or small-group leaders at your church and thinks, "Humph! I could never be like them. I just don't think quickly enough, and I never have the sort of questions that stimulate good small-group study." Don't beat yourself up about that. You need those study leaders, and they are a blessing to you. But guess what—they need you too! God has distinctively gifted, shaped, and formed you to be a blessing to all the other parts of your church. Recognize that, then, and "fan into flame" the gift that God *has* given you (2 Tim. 1:6).

The apostle Paul does teach that there is a relative priority of gifts. In 1 Corinthians 13, he emphasizes the primacy of love, and in chapter 14, he writes that he would "rather speak five intelligible words to instruct others than ten thousand words in a tongue" (v. 19). Gifts that instruct others, including Word-ministry gifts, are of crucial importance.

Word-ministry gifts are not limited to preaching, however. The COVID-19 pandemic highlighted the importance of the technological gifts (audiovisual and livestreaming) that enabled the Word of God to go out in times of crisis. We need to rediscover the value of harnessing creative gifts in visual art and the performing arts to communicate the unchanging truths of God's Word in our ever-changing world. In short, we need to develop a broader appreciation of how God has lavished a diversity of gifts on his church for the common good. To the extent that we fail to see this, the whole church will be impoverished.

Indeed, the necessity of our many gifts is demonstrated not just by the metaphor of the church as a body but also by the imagery of the church as a bride, building, business, and family. A diversity of gifts in all of these settings enhances the pursuit of a common purpose.

Making It Personal

1. What biblical metaphor do you most readily associate with the church? Why? How has it helped you to love the church? How could it be unhelpful if it is isolated from the other images of the church in Scripture?
2. Where have you seen unhealthy homogeneity in the church? What gifts are you tempted to undervalue or overvalue?
3. What gifts do you have that you could use to serve the church? How are you using them? How could they be maximized?
4. How does the church, diverse but united, fulfill its purpose? Take some time to reflect on the beauty of the church and thank God for the diverse but unified body of believers of which you're a part.
5. What can you do this week, practically, to encourage someone who is serving your church with a gift that usually goes noticed?

16

ONE CHURCH WITH TWO GENDERS

> *The Bible insists that men and women are equal in dignity and honor but distinct in role within marriage and the church. This distinction makes us inseparable because we need one another in order to glorify God and flourish.*

In Genesis 1, we read that God created humanity in his own image and that he created them "male and female" (Gen. 1:27). This tells us two incredibly important things.

First, as we saw in chapter 4, the language of "likeness" and "image" connotes royalty. Of all God's creatures, humanity has particular dignity because God made us to commune with himself (likeness) and to represent him in the world (image). This dignity is shared equally by men and women. It is difficult to overstate how revolutionary this is for any society—past or present—that does not see women as equal in value to men.

Second, and just as significant for our culture today, God established a distinction within humanity: "Male and female he created them" (Gen. 1:27). According to the Bible, gender is not a social construct. It is a binary, biological distinction that God has written into the created order.

In this chapter, we will examine gender in the context of the church, but, to understand the challenges we currently face, it is necessary first to consider gender within society at large.

Gender Confusion and Separation

Fifty years ago, the idea that gender is a binary, biological distinction would have been uncontroversial. Biological sex and gender were long understood to be precisely aligned. The same cannot be said today.

Perhaps the best illustration of this shift has been the recent furor surrounding comments made by J. K. Rowling, the author of the *Harry Potter* series. In 2019, a researcher named Maya Forstater was fired by the Center for Global Development after she posted gender-critical views on Twitter. These included the claim that a person cannot change their biological sex.[1] J. K. Rowling used her own Twitter account to voice her support for Forstater, writing that, while transgender people should be free to live their lives in "peace and security," women should not be "force[d] out of their jobs for stating that sex is real."[2] This triggered an avalanche of criticism, in which Rowling was accused of transphobia and labeled as a TERF (trans-exclusionary radical feminist).

Perhaps the most prominent criticism of Rowling's views came from Daniel Radcliffe, the actor who played Harry Potter in the 2001 film franchise. In an essay posted on the website of the Trevor Project, he wrote, "Transgender women are women. Any statement to the contrary erases the identity and dignity of transgender people."[3]

Classical Feminism: Distinct and Separate

The J. K. Rowling controversy illustrates a fascinating shift that has occurred in contemporary discussions of gender. In the twentieth century, feminist thinkers were committed to challenging gender stereotypes that artificially limited opportunities for women and reinforced cultural

---

1. Forstater was ultimately successful in her claim for unlawful discrimination by her employer. See Rachel Cooke, "'Now other women are free to say what they believe': researcher who lost her job over transgender tweets," *The Guardian*, July 10, 2022, https://www.theguardian.com/society/2022/jul/10/maya-forstater-transgender-tweets-tribunal-ruling.

2. Gwen Aviles, "J.K. Rowling faces backlash after tweeting support for 'transphobic' researcher," *NBC News*, December 19, 2019, https://www.nbcnews.com/feature/nbc-out/j-k-rowling-faces-backlash-after-tweeting-support-transphobic-researcher-n1104971.

3. Kinzi Sparks, "Daniel Radcliffe Responds to J.K. Rowling's Tweets on Gender Identity," Trevor Project, June 8, 2020, https://www.thetrevorproject.org/blog/daniel-radcliffe-responds-to-j-k-rowlings-tweets-on-gender-identity/.

expectations about their dress, role, and character. They distinguished sex from gender, arguing that "gender" is a social construct that facilitates the oppression of women.

| Male | Female |

Fig. 16.1. Classical Feminism—Distinct and Separate

Helen Joyce writes that historically feminists viewed "sex [a]s a biological category, and gender [as] a historical category; sex is why women are oppressed, and gender is *how* women are oppressed."[4] Thus, feminists acknowledged and celebrated a fundamental distinction between men and women but rejected the view that this distinction either limited opportunities for women or required them to comply with particular cultural norms and expectations.

More recently, radical feminism has gone further, arguing that women are not merely equal to men but superior to them. That was the claim of Emory University anthropologist Melvin Konner, who wrote, "Women are not equal to men; they are superior in many ways, and in most ways that will count in the future."[5]

This view is not limited to academia. In popular discourse, it may be seen in the comments of Christine Lagarde, the former head of the International Monetary Fund, on the tenth anniversary of the 2008 financial crash. She wrote, "If it had been Lehman Sisters rather than Lehman Brothers, the world might well look a lot different today."[6] In a similar vein, Boris Johnson suggested in 2022 that Vladimir Putin's invasion of Ukraine was "a perfect

---

4. Helen Joyce, *Trans: When Ideology Meets Reality* (London: Oneworld, 2021), 2.
5. Melvin Konner, "The End of Male Supremacy," *Chronicle of Higher Education*, March 30, 2015, https://www.chronicle.com/article/the-end-of-male-supremacy/.
6. Christine Lagarde, "Ten Years After Lehman—Lessons Learned and Challenges Ahead," *IMFBlog*, September 5, 2018. Quoted in Douglas Murray, *The Madness of Crowds: Gender, Race and Identity* (London: Bloomsbury, 2019), 80.

example of toxic masculinity" and would not have happened had Putin been a woman.[7]

Today, it is not uncommon to attribute some of the most horrific acts to maleness or masculinity and to use this framing of events (identity politics) to pit the genders against each other. One of the most harrowing examples in recent times followed the kidnap, rape, and murder of Sarah Everard by a Metropolitan Police officer on March 3, 2021. It was a horrific crime and rightly scandalized the United Kingdom. Some individuals and groups, however, framed it as emblematic of the way men treat women in general. One well-wisher who had experienced abuse at the hands of a man even left a tribute note that read, "What happened to you happened to me."

Now, we need to be clear that the majority of violent criminals are male (82 percent, according to the 2020 Crime Survey for England and Wales)[8] and that women are twice as likely to experience domestic abuse than men.[9] Sin clearly causes men to abuse their unique power over women, and we should seek to counter and mitigate such abuse. It is, however, deeply divisive to focus on specific, horrific crimes and then impute the evil therein to men or masculinity in general. This simply drives a wedge between men and women that makes matters worse.

Transgenderism: Inseparable and Indistinct

If radical feminism acknowledges a fundamental distinction between men and women but embraces this distinction to the point of separation, transgenderism does the opposite.[10] It suggests that a person is a man or a woman based

---

7. Interview with German media at the G7 Summit in Schloss Elmau. Reported in Nadeem Badshah, "Boris Johnson: Putin would not have invaded Ukraine if he were a woman," *The Guardian*, June 28, 2022, https://www.theguardian.com/world/2022/jun/29/boris-johnson-claims-putin-would-not-have-invaded-ukraine-if-he-was-a-woman.

8. Office for National Statistics, *Crime Survey for England and Wales: Year Ending March 2020*, accessed November 28, 2023, https://www.ons.gov.uk/peoplepopulationandcommunity/crimeandjustice/articles/thenatureofviolentcrimeinenglandandwales/yearendingmarch2020.

9. Office for National Statistics, *Domestic Abuse in England and Wales: Year Ending March 2018*, https://www.ons.gov.uk/peoplepopulationandcommunity/crimeandjustice/bulletins/domesticabuseinenglandandwales/yearendingmarch2018.

10. Transgenderism should be distinguished from transsexualism. *Transgender* is an umbrella term that includes all people who have chosen a gender that differs from their gender "assigned at birth" (determined by genital features and chromosomes). *Transsexual* is a more specific term that refers to a person whose genitals or other sexual characteristics

purely on how they feel rather than on their biology. This, ironically, undoes many of the efforts of twentieth-century classical feminism to deconstruct gender stereotypes. After all, what does it mean to *feel* like a woman except to embrace a social construction of femininity (be it one of your own making or of someone else's)? As Rebecca McLaughlin puts it, "if our bodies are removed from the equation, those stereotypes are all we have left."[11]

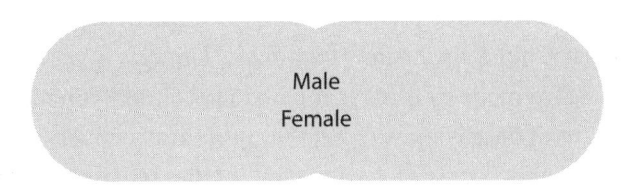

Male
Female

Fig. 16.2. Transgenderism—Indistinct and Inseparable

Reducing gender to a matter of subjective self-identification based on fluid stereotypes inevitably removes any meaningful distinction between the genders. Gender is no longer a matter of fixed "hardware"—it has become "software" that we may change at will.

This has alarming implications. For example, consider that, historically, the intentional exposure of one's genitals (exhibitionism) and observation of naked people (voyeurism) have been considered sex crimes in the United Kingdom, when done without the consent of the other party or parties involved. It has also historically been understood that, when a person enters a changing room, they implicitly consent to be seen in a state of undress by the other occupants. Previously, most people gave this consent based on the assumption that the other occupants of the changing room would be of the same biological sex. Now that gender has become legally redefined independent of biological sex, it is no longer possible for a person to consent to being seen only by people of the same biological sex. In other words, a person's right to use the changing room of their self-identified gender has

have been changed either through surgery or hormone treatment. I am using the umbrella term *transgender* in this chapter.
    11. Rebecca McLaughlin, *The Secular Creed: Engaging Five Contemporary Claims* (Austin: The Gospel Coalition, 2021), 86.

trumped the right of other occupants not to be victims of what was previously defined as a sex crime.[12] In a similar vein, biologically male prisoners who identify as female, including rapists and murderers, are now being transferred to female-only prisons.[13]

The erosion of gender distinction has even brought prominent members of the gay rights movement into conflict with trans activists. For example, Fred Sargeant, who organized the first ever Gay Pride march in the United States, posted on Twitter, "Homosexuality is same-sex attraction. Biological sex is real. Sex is binary, not a spectrum."[14] Similarly, Douglas Murray wrote that "many of the claims made by trans [people] do not simply run in contravention to the claims of the gay movement; they profoundly undermine them."[15]

Indeed, gay rights activists have long fought the stereotype that gay men are effeminate and that lesbian women are masculine—they believe this is outmoded, prejudiced, and homophobic. The transgender movement, however, "keeps suggesting that people who are slightly effeminate or don't like the right sports are not merely gay but potentially inhabiting the wrong body and are in fact men, or women, inside."[16]

Over the past fifty years, Western culture has leapt from distinguishing the genders—separating them in the process—to removing any distinction between them at all. This has been societally disruptive, especially for the young, who have to cope with the vastly differing ideologies that are being thrown their way. One thing that seems to unite feminists, gay activists, and trans activists, however, is the view that the biblical understanding of gender is outdated and repressive. It is to this that we must now turn.

Male and Female as Distinct but Inseparable

We have seen that the Bible's starting point for understanding sex and gender is Genesis 1:27: "In the image of God he created them; male and female he created them." This verse establishes a couple of things: (1) the

---

12. See Joyce, *Trans*, 159.
13. See Joyce, 160.
14. Fred Sargeant, https://twitter.com/FredSargeant. Quoted in McLaughlin, *The Secular Creed*, 88.
15. Murray, *The Madness of Crowds*, 209.
16. Murray, 209.

inherent and equal dignity of men and women, and (2) the fundamental distinction between men and women. The former point is often taken for granted in our society, yet it is has not been self-evident throughout history. British historian Tom Holland writes, "That every human being possessed an equal dignity was not remotely self-evident a truth. A Roman would have laughed at it.... The origins of this principle—as Nietzsche had so contemptuously pointed out—lay not in the French Revolution, nor in the Declaration of Independence, nor in the Enlightenment, but in the Bible."[17]

We are so used to hearing secular accusations that Christianity is unenlightened and misogynistic that we are in danger of actually believing them. In reality, however, the worldview that enables these accusations is itself Christian. Holland continues, "Any condemnation of Christianity as patriarchal and repressive derived from a framework of values that was itself utterly Christian."[18] In other words, Christianity grounds the equal rights of men and women, which is the necessary foundation for critiquing the oppression of women by men. Given this, we do well to ask why Christianity is so often accused of being patriarchal and repressive.

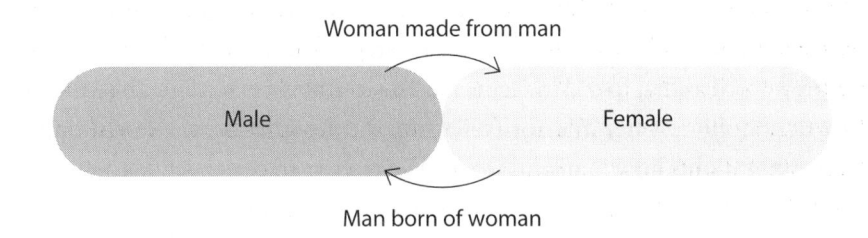

Woman made from man

Male   Female

Man born of woman

Male and female both necessary for human flourishing

Fig. 16.3. Biblical View—Distinct and Inseparable

As we saw in part 4, there is a fundamental difference between how our culture understands identity and how the Bible defines it. In our culture,

---

17. Tom Holland, *Dominion: How the Christian Revolution Remade the World* (New York: Basic Books, 2019), 494.
18. Holland, 532.

identity is found internally and is validated externally as we express it through personal action; our identity is earned rather than ascribed. The Bible teaches the exact opposite: our identity is found externally. We are valuable as human beings because we have been made in the image of God, and we are now called to live out that reality. Identity is ascribed, not earned.

It is difficult to overstate the significance of this difference. The cry of our culture is "you are what you do." The Bible replies, "No, you do what you are." We saw this in part 2 through our discussion of the creation mandate. Human beings have been created in God's image to represent him in the world. This means continuing his creative work of ordering and filling the earth. Because we are God's image bearers, we do his creative work. We do what we are.

Further, the Bible teaches that our identity as male and female determines our roles in two important and closely linked relationships: marriage and the church. Even back in Genesis 2, there is a hint at this distinction. The woman is taken from Adam—from his rib—hinting that she is necessary to complement him (see Gen. 2:22–23). Accordingly, Scripture calls her Adam's "helper" (Gen. 2:18).

It is important to realize that "helper" is not a demeaning title. Elsewhere, in Psalm 115:9, the *Lord* is described as Israel's "help" using the very same Hebrew word as that found in Genesis 2:18—certainly, extending this label to Eve does not imply her inferiority. Rather, the designation of Eve as Adam's helper highlights how man and woman were created equal yet distinct, that they may complement each other in certain relationships.

Distinct but Inseparable in Marriage

The first of those relationships between men and women is marriage. In Ephesians 5:22–33, the apostle Paul teaches that marriage is a picture of Christ's relationship to the church. Wives are called to submit to their husbands "as the church submits to Christ" (Eph. 5:24). The word Paul uses for "submit" describes a voluntary action. Submission within marriage is to be given, not coerced, just as the church willingly submits to Christ. Alongside this submission, husbands are called to love their wives "just as Christ loved the church and gave himself up for her" (Eph. 5:25). The example for husbands is Christ's self-sacrificial love for the church.

Some claim that Ephesians 5 facilitates oppressive power dynamics within marriage due to its command for wives to submit to their husbands. Nothing could be further from the truth, however. Leadership, according to the apostle Paul, is not about power and domination—it's about service and self-sacrifice.

When we read passages like Ephesians 5 today, we often run into problems, as we tend to view relationships in terms of function and assume a meritocracy. So, when we read that wives must submit to their husbands, we assume that this includes decisions about where to live, how to parent, and which movie to watch tonight. Restricted to this sphere of activity, we rightly ask: How can that be fair or right? What if the wife is smarter, or wiser, or a better judge of movies? Wouldn't it be better for her to make the decisions in those situations?

This is to completely misunderstand the nature of headship within marriage. Headship is not about who makes the decisions but about the framing of the relationship itself. The distinction is not based on competency or status but rather on order. God has established an order in creation between a husband and a wife. We don't understand the reason why he did this, but we trust that it is good.

Gives himself up for her

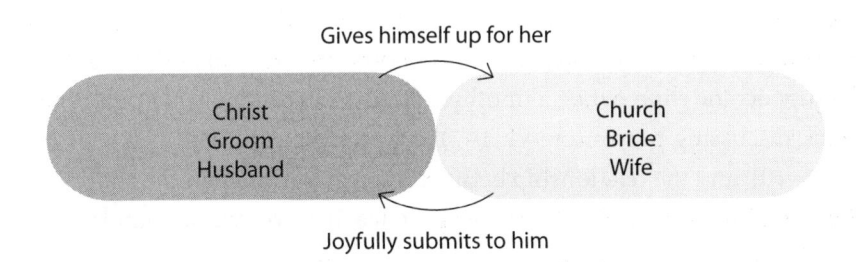

Christ
Groom
Husband

Church
Bride
Wife

Joyfully submits to him

Fig. 16.4. Christ and the Church—Distinct and Inseparable

Just as the distinction of function within the Trinity (described by theologians as the "economic Trinity") does not imply that the Son is inferior to the Father, the distinction of function within the family does not imply that a wife is inferior to her husband. Our problem is that we assume that "we are what we do," whereas the Bible insists that "we do what we are." This is why God the Father sends and God the Son goes. It is why a husband self-sacrificially leads and a wife willingly submits, regardless of who is the most able and competent. God has written these inseparable distinctions into the relationship of marriage, and they are for the complementary good of the family as a whole.

Distinct but Inseparable in the Church

How are we to understand the distinction between men and women in the church? It is important to acknowledge that this is a controversial subject. Bible-believing Christians disagree with one another. The starting point, however, must be a recognition of the close connection between the nuclear family and the church.

As we have seen, the family is one of several metaphors that the New Testament uses to describe the church. Christians are brothers and sisters. They are to treat older men as fathers and younger men as brothers; older women as mothers and younger women as sisters (see 1 Tim. 5:1–2). The New Testament also establishes a parallel between a husband's headship of his wife and the elders' headship of the church. It does so in a number of places, but we will focus on 1 Timothy 2. Here, Paul roots his teaching in creation, which confirms that it applies not only to his original audience but also to the church in general.

Paul is writing to his apprentice, Timothy, whom he has left in Ephesus to support the church. In 1 Timothy 2, he gives instructions for public worship, discussing prayer (see vv. 1–7), appropriate dress and behavior (see vv. 8–10), and the relationship between men and women in the church. He then writes, "I do not permit a woman to teach or to assume authority over a man; she must be quiet" (v. 12).

Unsurprisingly, this has proven to be a controversial verse. It is possible that Paul is prohibiting women from engaging in two distinct activities: (1) teaching in the church, and (2) assuming authority over men in the church.[19] Alternatively, the connecting word between "teach" and "assume authority" may suggest that Paul is combining the verbs to express a single

---

19. Andreas J. Köstenberger, "A Complex Sentence: The Syntax of 1 Timothy 2:12," in *Women in the Church: A Fresh Analysis of 1 Timothy 2:9–15*, ed. Andreas J. Köstenberger, Thomas R. Schreiner, and H. Scott Baldwin (Grand Rapids: Baker, 1995), 81–103.

idea: teaching with authority over men.[20] Either way, it is clear that women are not permitted to teach with authority over men in the local church. Paul confirms this later when he insists that the teaching office of elder in the church is open only to men (see 1 Tim. 3:2; 5:17).

Readers may still ask, *why*? If women are as competent to teach and lead as men, why shouldn't they lead in the church? Paul gives the reason in the verses that follow, and it is fascinating to see how his reasoning maps onto the pattern of redemptive history that we examined in part 2.

Paul begins with creation (see v. 13) and the order established in creation. As we have seen, the six days of creation involved ordering and filling. That ordering included the ordering of the relationship between Adam and Eve, which is then to be replicated in every single marriage. The fall, however, disrupted this order: "And Adam was not the one deceived; it was the woman who was deceived and became a sinner" (v. 14).

Some Christians struggle with this verse. Is Paul really saying that men must lead the church because the first person to give in to Satan was a woman? I don't think so. His point is that the created order was disrupted in the fall. Adam should have been lovingly leading his wife in the garden of Eden—instead, he was twiddling his thumbs when Satan came calling. Rather than lovingly and firmly reminding Eve of God's command (see Gen. 2:16–17), Adam simply went along with her rebellion (see 3:6). And when God comes calling, he shirks responsibility and blames his wife (see v. 12). A breakdown of the divine order in marriage lies behind the fall.

Wonderfully, however, redemption comes through a restoration of the divine order. Commentators disagree regarding what Paul teaches in 1 Timothy 2:15, which reads, "But women will be saved through childbearing." According to some, Paul teaches that women will be saved physically from the perils of childbirth; according to others, Paul teaches that they will be saved spiritually by returning to their feminine role as child-bearers. Neither explanation is particularly satisfactory, as they both depart from the normal

20. See Craig L. Blomberg, "Neither Hierarchicalist nor Egalitarian: Gender Roles in Paul," in *Two Views on Women in Ministry*, ed. James R. Beck and Craig L. Blomberg, Counterpoints (Grand Rapids: Zondervan, 2001), 329–72; Philip B. Payne, "1 Tim 2.12 and the Use of ουδε to Combine Two Elements to Express a Single Idea," *New Testament Studies* 54, no. 2 (April 2008): 235–53 (an egalitarian whose conclusions I do not follow). For a contrary view, see Köstenberger, "A Complex Sentence: The Syntax of 1 Timothy 2:12."

New Testament usage of the verb "to save." It seems far more likely that Paul is referring to the spiritual salvation that comes through the birth of Jesus—the Messiah.[21]

The imagery in this verse is beautiful. Eve was created to be fruitful and life-giving as she fulfilled her God-given role in the created order. The fall disrupted that divine order, and Eve brought forth death instead. In the incarnation, however, the order was restored, and Mary, a descendant of Eve, became life-giving again as she brought forth a Savior for all who live in faith, love, holiness, and self-control.

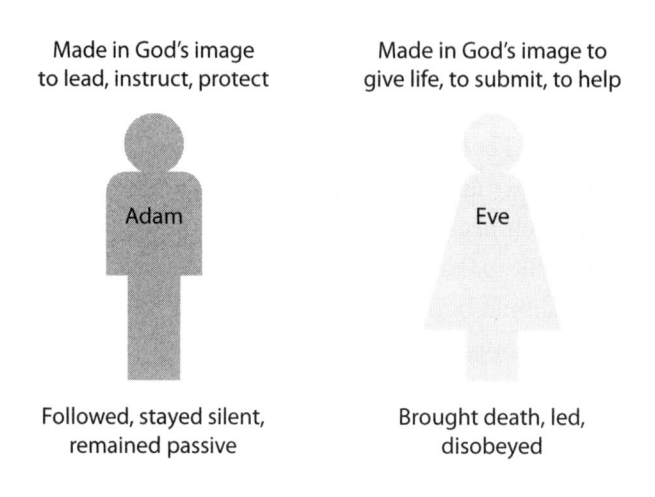

Made in God's image to lead, instruct, protect	Made in God's image to give life, to submit, to help
Adam	Eve
Followed, stayed silent, remained passive	Brought death, led, disobeyed

Fig. 16.5. The Disruption of the Fall

In sum, God has established an order within the church. Like the order in marriage, and like the order in the Godhead, this order is good—but it is not meritocratic. The CEO of a company is appointed based on their skills, experience, and ability to lead. The qualifications for the leaders of a church are quite different. First Timothy 3 and Titus 1 provide extensive lists of such qualifications. Only one of those qualifications relates to competency: the ability to teach (see 1 Tim. 3:2). The rest are character-based. This means that

---

21. See George W. Knight III, *The Pastoral Epistles*, The New International Greek Testament Commentary (Milton Keynes, UK: Paternoster Press, 1992), 146–48.

those who lead the church are not necessarily the best teachers in the church, the best leaders in the church, or even the godliest members of the church. They are simply those who have met Scripture's character qualifications and who have been recognized by the church as having done so.

In addition, because the church is a spiritual family, God has ordained that churches should be led by men alone. This is the order he has established in his wisdom, and even though we may not fully understand why he did so, the order is good.

God has made men and women distinct but inseparable. They need each other, and they depend on each other. When the God-given order is observed, it is truly beautiful. This does not mean that women submit to all men in the church. That is nowhere taught in the Bible. Rather, women are called to lovingly and willingly submit to their own husbands and to those men who have been appointed to serve as elders of the church—elders to whom their husbands must submit as well.

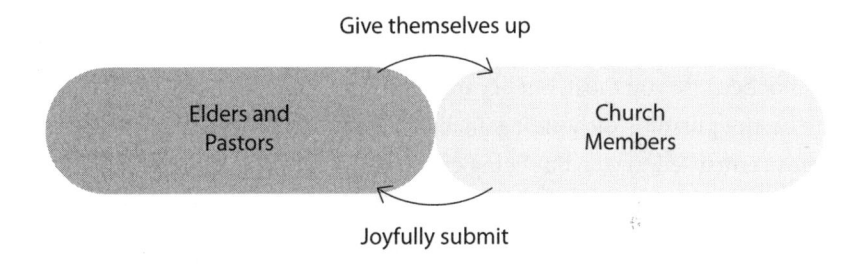

Give themselves up

Elders and Pastors   Church Members

Joyfully submit

Fig. 16.6. Leaders and Members in the Church—Distinct and Inseparable

Living It Out: Beautiful Complementarity

Radical feminism distinguishes men and women to the point of separation, pitting the genders against each other. Transgenderism erases the distinction and makes gender a matter of subjective choice, which is forever unstable. The Bible insists that men and women are equal in dignity and honor but distinct in role within marriage and the church. This distinction makes us inseparable because we need each other in order to image God as one—which, as we saw in part 2, means bringing order and flourishing to the world.

Wouldn't it be great if we could regain this vision? We live in an age where everybody wants to be a leader. Some desire power, others want control, still others hunger for approval. Our culture tells us that "we are what we do." If you are a leader in business or the community, you should be admired and served. The Bible's picture of leadership is very different.

When the mother of James and John asked Jesus to give special leadership roles to her sons, Jesus replied, "You don't know what you are asking" (Matt. 20:22). She assumed that the roles would confer status and honor on her sons, but Jesus knew they would actually confer suffering. The problem was that James and John's mother was thinking like the Gentiles, who assumed that leadership is all about lording power over others and using it for your own advantage. Jesus teaches that leadership is really all about service: "Whoever wants to become great among you must be your servant . . . just as the Son of Man did not come to be served, but to serve, and to give his life as a ransom for many" (vv. 26–28). These words clearly stuck with the apostle Peter, because many years later, he wrote the following to his fellow elders:

> Be shepherds of God's flock that is under your care, watching over them —not because you must, but because you are willing, as God wants you to be; not pursuing dishonest gain, but eager to serve; not lording it over those entrusted to you, but being examples to the flock. (1 Peter 5:2–3)

We need to restore a biblical understanding of leadership and complementarity within the church. Order is a good gift from God. We do not need to fully understand it in order to affirm that it is good and beautiful.

A few years ago, we were joined at City Church by a Mission to the World missionary in her seventies. Barbara is far wiser than I, she knows her Bible better, and she has far more life experience than any of our church elders. Throughout her time at City Church, Barbara has lovingly supported and encouraged our elders. She has frequently given me advice, and I have always benefited from it. Yet she has always submitted to the elders of the church. Barbara has modelled beautiful complementarity for us.

Those who are called to lead, whether in marriage or the church, must grasp that leadership is about radical service and self-sacrifice. And when we are called to submit, whether we be men or women, we must recognize that it is no more demeaning than Jesus submitting to his heavenly Father. It is an opportunity to glorify the distinct yet inseparable God through his distinct yet inseparable church.

Making It Personal

1. What view of gender and gender expectations were you taught as a child? How has that shaped your understanding of your own role?
2. Where have you seen and heard unhealthy gender stereotypes in society? In the church? How has this impacted you personally?
3. What is the most prevalent view of gender and gender expectations in your circle of friends? Why do you think that is?
5. What do you think about biblical complementarity? What about this view do you find beautiful? What do you struggle most to accept? Why do you think that is?
6. If you are uncomfortable with biblical complementarity, how could you wrestle with that discomfort in a God-pleasing way? What do you want to understand better? With whom could you discuss these things?
7. In what ways might those struggles affect your experience of the church? Of dating, marriage, divorce, and widowhood? Of being single?

17

ONE CHURCH OF ALL NATIONS

> *God saved us to be one united people—distinct in our ethnic and cultural backgrounds but inseparable in our worship of him. The church must pursue unity in ethnic and cultural diversity because it is an outworking of the gospel.*

Martin Luther King Jr. famously said that Sunday morning at 11 a.m. is the most segregated hour in the United States. Tragically, that is still true in many parts of the nation and, indeed, the world. There are Black churches, White churches, Hispanic churches, Chinese churches, Korean churches, and Nigerian churches. Is this really a problem, though? Is it possible that monoethnic and monocultural churches actually serve the mission of the church better than diverse churches?

In the mid to late twentieth century, Donald McGavran, professor of church growth at Fuller Theological Seminary, developed what is known as the "homogenous unit principle." He argued that the central purpose of missions is to see the lost won for Christ. We have a responsibility to allocate resources for missions in a way that maximizes this outcome, and so we need to prioritize making disciples over perfecting disciples. This means we ought to remove some of the obstacles that stand in the way of people following Jesus.

McGavran noted that "people like to become Christians without crossing racial, linguistic or class barriers."[1] It is social factors, not theological obstacles, that prevent people from turning to Christ.[2] Therefore, if we want to see the church grow rapidly, we need to focus on homogeneous units, so that people can come to Christ without leaving behind their culture, language, or class.

Pragmatically, this may appear sensible. College students seem to be better at reaching their peers, so perhaps we should plant churches just for college students. African Americans find it easier to attend a Black church than a White church. So, for the sake of the gospel, isn't it right to have Black churches that are intentionally homogeneous, even if they do not explicitly exclude non-Blacks? And, by implication, isn't it okay to have intentionally White churches that seek to reach White people? Surely that would be the best allocation of limited resources—to separate churches along ethnic, socioeconomic, and cultural lines. Or would it?

Addressing Ethnic Prejudice

Before we tackle that question, it is important to consider the different ways in which Western society has sought to address ethnic prejudice. In a famous speech, Martin Luther King Jr. declared, "I have a dream that my four little children will one day live in a nation where they will not be judged by the color of their skin but by the content of their character. . . . I have a dream that . . . one day right down in Alabama little Black boys and Black girls will be able to join hands with little white boys and white girls as sisters and brothers."[3] At the height of the civil rights movement, King and his supporters longed for a nation where people judged you in terms of your character, not your skin color. On July 2, 1964, the Civil Rights Act was signed into law, and a new era of integration dawned.

---

1. Donald A. McGavran, *Understanding Church Growth*, 3rd ed. (Grand Rapids: Eerdmans, 1990), 163.
2. McGavran, 156.
3. "Read Martin Luther King Jr.'s 'I Have a Dream' speech in its entirety," National Public Radio, January 16, 2023, https://www.npr.org/2010/01/18/122701268/i-have-a-dream-speech-in-its-entirety.

Color Blindness: Denial of Distinction Leads to Separation

As the United States adapted to these changes, many began to embrace an attitude that might be described as "color blindness"—the insistence that ethnicity does not matter and that therefore we should be blind to the color of people's skin.

Instinctively, this is an appealing response to historic prejudice, but it is problematic for a number of reasons. First, it ignores and fails to respect people's distinctive ethnic and cultural heritage. Second, it can actually lead to the disruption of interracial relationships. Research has shown that an overemphasis on preventing relationships from going wrong can actually lead people to develop negative feelings about these relationships, leading to withdrawal. Third, color blindness can end up masking racism and leaving people insensitive to it. Assuming color blindness and refusing to notice people's ethnicities can make prejudice seem less plausible, which, in turn, can make such prejudice less likely to be detected.[4]

The attitude of color blindness, while well meaning, fails to acknowledge ethnic distinction and may actually lead to separation between people of different ethnicities. As the recording artist Shai Linne helpfully observes, "God was intentional when He gave me brown skin. He didn't give it to me that it might be ignored. He gave it to me that it would be appreciated and that He might be praised for His creative genius. So don't rob God of praise by ignoring it!"[5]

Identity Politics: Group Identity Leads to Separation

If the pursuit of color blindness has unintentionally led to ethnic separation, critical race theory has done the same thing more directly and intentionally. When I was a law student in the 1990s, critical legal studies was seen as a

---

4. See the research reviewed in Victoria C. Plaut, Kecia M. Thomas, Kyneshawau Hurd, and Celina A. Romano, "Do Color Blindness and Multiculturalism Remedy or Foster Discrimination and Racism?" *Current Directions in Psychological Science* 27, no. 3 (June 2018): 200–206, https://doi.org/10.1177/0963721418766068.

5. Shai Linne, *The New Reformation: Finding Hope in the Fight for Ethnic Unity* (Chicago: Moody Publishers, 2021), 133.

rather niche and obscure jurisprudential discipline. Today, it has become mainstream with the development of critical race theory (CRT).

At its heart, CRT claims that race[6] is a social construct and that racism includes not only individual prejudice but also systemic prejudice, as expressed in society's laws, institutions, and policies. CRT is surely right to insist that the sin of racism has not just remained in human hearts but infiltrated and distorted society's structures and institutions. It is exactly what we see in the book of Esther, for example, when the evil Haman convinces King Xerxes to enact legislation that would annihilate the Jews (Est. 3:7–14). We should be grateful to CRT for showing how racial prejudice spills over into society's structures and systems.

Unfortunately, it has gone further than that by artificially constructing group identities that equate race with culture and then pitting those ethnic groups against one another. This manifests itself in a number of potentially divisive concepts. The idea of "White privilege" has become popular and has led to "whiteness" trainings, whereby White employees are trained to understand their inherent biases. Although aspects of this training may be helpful, it conflates ethnicity and culture, wrongly assuming that all White people are shaped by the same cultural influences. It fails to acknowledge cultural nuances within ethnic groups and makes sweeping generalizations that can be harmful and divisive.

In a similar way, the concept of "cultural appropriation"—the unacknowledged adoption of the cultural practices of one social or ethnic group by the members of another—rightly sought to combat the terrible effects of colonialism. Today, however, it is often used to attack people who (haphazardly) seek to cross cultural boundaries.[7] A striking example of this

---

6. Throughout this chapter, outside of our discussion of CRT, we will speak of "ethnicity" rather than "race." CRT is right to say that race is a social construct used to perpetuate the idea that there are superior and inferior races. God only created one race: the human race. See Linne, *The New Reformation*, 107–9. For a contrary view, see Irwyn L. Ince Jr., *The Beautiful Community: Unity, Diversity, and the Church at Its Best* (Downers Grove, IL: IVP, 2020), 76–77.

7. To be clear, I am not suggesting that Jamie Oliver's recipe was inoffensive to Jamaicans. See Vaughn Stafford Gray, "A Brief History of Jamaican Jerk," *Smithsonian Magazine*, December 22, 2020, www.smithsonianmag.com/arts-culture/brief-history-jamaican-jerk-180976597/. My concern is that this controversy was addressed using the freighted language of "cultural appropriation."

was the criticism leveled at celebrity chef Jamie Oliver for his "punchy jerk rice" recipe. Labour MP Dawn Butler tweeted her disapproval, insisting that "this appropriation from Jamaica needs to stop."[8]

Modern identity politics assumes that a person's views and assumptions are based on their group identity (namely, their ethnicity, gender, and/or sexuality).[9] It then sets these groups against one another using the frame of power dynamics, whereby one group is portrayed as the oppressor and the other as the oppressed.[10] This framing of ethnic identities is undoubtedly based on an accurate observation of historical patterns. The evidence for the systemic oppression of Blacks by Whites in the British Empire, the Americas, and apartheid South Africa is undeniable. However, in making broad generalizations and in conflating ethnicity with culture and politics, identity politics falls into the very error it seeks to address. It not only distinguishes ethnic groups but also pits them against one another.

We have seen that the "color blindness" approach to addressing ethnic prejudice fails to properly distinguish ethnicities and that the "identity politics" approach separates them and stokes animosity. Is there a better way?

One People of Many Ethnicities: Distinct but Inseparable

A brief overview of Scripture reveals that God always intended to call to himself a united yet diverse people.[11] Genesis 10 describes how the multitude of nations descended from Noah's sons, and Genesis 11 shows how these nations were then scattered over the face of the earth following

---

8. Dawn Butler, "#jamieoliver @jamieoliver #jerk," Twitter, August 18, 2018, 10:02 a.m., https://twitter.com/dawnbutlerbrent/status/1030741609984548864.

9. For a recent example, see the comments made by Member of Parliament Rupa Huq. She called Kwasi Kwarteng—the then-newly appointed chancellor of the exchequer—"superficially" black following his announcement of radical tax cuts. Regardless of the merits of Kwarteng's proposal (he was subsequently forced to resign, bringing down Liz Truss's government!), it is clearly wrong to suggest that a particular fiscal position is incompatible with being black. See "Rupa Huq MP apologises for 'superficially' black remark," *BBC News*, September 28, 2022, https://www.bbc.co.uk/news/uk-politics-63050482.

10. See Jonathan Leeman, "Identity Politics and the Death of Christian Unity," *9Marks*, April 15, 2020, https://www.9marks.org/article/identity-politics-and-the-death-of-christian-unity/.

11. See also Rebecca McLaughlin's excellent and more detailed overview in Rebecca McLaughlin, *The Secular Creed: Engaging Five Contemporary Claims* (Austin: The Gospel Coalition, 2021), 8–16.

the construction of the Tower of Babel (see Gen. 11:8–9). Irwyn Ince Jr. graphically describes the consequences of this episode as the ghettoization of humanity.[12]

Just one chapter later, we read about God's incredible plan to reverse this ghettoization by forming one new people out of these diverse nations. He appears to Abram and promises to make him into a "great nation," assuring him that "all peoples on earth will be blessed through [him]" (Gen. 12:2–3). Later, in Genesis 17:5, God renames Abram: "No longer will you be called Abram; your name will be Abraham, for I have made you a father of many nations."

The rest of the Old Testament chronicles the beginning of this process. God fulfills his promise to make Abraham into a great nation and brings the people of Israel out of slavery in Egypt. Right from the start, people from other nations are added to God's people, and the nations are blessed through them. Moses marries a Midianite named Zipporah (see Exod. 2:11–21). A Canaanite prostitute named Rahab helps the Israelites and is welcomed into God's people (see Josh. 2). A Moabite named Ruth pledges her allegiance to her mother-in-law Naomi: "Where you go I will go, and where you stay I will stay. Your people will be my people and your God my God" (Ruth 1:16). Ruth herself is the great-grandmother of King David (see Ruth 4:21–22). David's son builds the temple in Jerusalem, and God declares the temple to be "a house of prayer for all nations" (Isa. 56:7).

We have to wait until the New Testament to see exactly how God's plan is brought to fruition. In his letter to the Galatians, the apostle Paul writes,

> Understand, then, that those who have faith are children of Abraham. Scripture foresaw that God would justify the Gentiles by faith, and announced the gospel in advance to Abraham: "All nations will be blessed through you." So those who rely on faith are blessed along with Abraham, the man of faith. (Gal. 3:7–9)

This explains how Abraham, the father of one nation—the Jews—could also be the father of many nations, just as Genesis 17:5 promised. We are his

12. Ince Jr., 69–81.

children through our faith in Jesus Christ. Abraham believed God, and it was "credited to him as righteousness" (Gal. 3:6). That same faith is available to non-Jews—Gentiles—because Jesus died for both Jew and Gentile. As Paul writes elsewhere, the gospel "is the power of God that brings salvation to everyone who believes: first to the Jew, then to the Gentile" (Rom. 1:16).

Jesus's blood "purchased for God persons from every tribe and language and people and nation" (Rev. 5:9). This is the "gospel" that was preached to Abraham, according to Galatians 3:8: the glorious good news that, in Christ, God is forming a multinational, multiethnic, multilingual people for his glory.

Jesus's genealogy confirms his own mixed ethnic ancestry, featuring both Rahab the Canaanite and Ruth the Moabite (see Matt. 1:5). In his ministry, he deliberately mixed with ethnic outsiders: the Samaritan woman (see John 4), the Roman centurion (see Matt. 8:5–13), and the Syrophoenician woman (see Mark 7:24–29). And in his teaching, Jesus made a despised Samaritan the hero in his famous parable (see Luke 10:25–37).

The gospels proclaim that Jesus came to redeem people of all nations, which is confirmed by his Great Commission at the end of Matthew's account: "All authority in heaven and on earth has been given to me. Therefore go and make disciples of all nations, baptizing them in the name of the Father and of the Son and of the Holy Spirit" (Matt. 28:18–19). The word translated as "nations" (as in Gal. 3:8) is *ethne,* meaning all ethno-linguistic groups. The disciples are called to help people from every ethnicity become followers of Christ through faith.

This is exactly what happens in the book of Acts. The events of Acts 2 are like a reversal of the Tower of Babel. The nations (people from all over North Africa and the Middle East) are gathered in Jerusalem for the Feast of Pentecost when suddenly Peter and the other apostles are empowered to speak in foreign languages so that the people are able to hear them declaring the wonders of God in their native tongues (see Acts 2:11). Notice that the apostles are miraculously gifted to speak in foreign languages and that their listeners are not miraculously gifted to understand Aramaic or Greek.

God did not intend to make one homogeneous people group with the same language, ethnicity, and culture. Rather, he intended to create one new people for his glory, comprising believers from every tribe, tongue, and nation—distinct but inseparable. This is what comes to pass in the chapters that follow. Samaritans come to faith in Acts 8:4–25, and then an Ethiopian eunuch is baptized by the side of a road in Acts 8:26–40. Two chapters later, Peter is ordered to preach the gospel to a Roman centurion named Cornelius. After seeing the man's conversion, Peter declares, "I now realize how true it is that God does not show favoritism but accepts from every nation the one who fears him and does what is right" (Acts 10:34–35).

Before we get even halfway through the book of Acts, the gospel has reached the third largest city in the Roman Empire, Antioch. A church has been planted there (see Acts 11:19–30), and Acts 13 offers a glorious glimpse of this congregation's diverse leadership as it gathers to worship, fast, and seek the Lord. Lucius, we're told, was from modern-day Libya; Barnabas from Cyprus (according to Acts 4:36), Simeon was called Niger ("black"), hinting at his ethnicity; and Manaen was from the upper echelons of Jewish society, having been raised in Herod's palace (see Acts 13:1). The leadership in Antioch was gloriously diverse, both ethnically and socially. For the first time, a local church started to look like the universal church for which Christ had shed his blood.

The full glory of that universal church is revealed in the closing chapters of the Bible as John beholds this vision:

> After this I looked, and there before me was a great multitude that no one could count, from every nation, tribe, people and language, standing before the throne and before the Lamb. They were wearing white robes and were holding palm branches in their hands. And they cried out in a loud voice: "Salvation belongs to our God, who sits on the throne, and to the Lamb." (Rev. 7:9–10)

This is where the universe is heading: one people—a single multitude—united in purpose as it worships the one Lamb, and yet utterly diverse in terms of ethnicity, language, background, and culture. This is true unity in diversity. It is what politicians, sociologists, and even John Lennon longed for. Lennon thought that it could be achieved through an atheistic, socialist utopia. The twentieth century showed that to be naive—such a vision simply leads to further corruption, lying, despair, conflict, and bloodshed. We need a foundation built on righteousness, leading to peace and joy in the Holy Spirit (see Rom 14:17).[13] Jesus Christ has built this foundation. He has created in himself one diverse people—distinct but inseparable.

The Source of Unity in Diversity

Recently my dad was sharing our family history with me. He is now in his seventies, but it was the first time we had discussed in any detail my grandfather and his parents—all of whom died before I was born. As my dad spoke to me, he began to recite from his own father's diaries. It was fascinating. One entry from the 1940s said matter-of-factly, "Bomb landed on neighboring street last night. The whole family were killed," and then continued, "Went for a dance at the Palais this evening." The diaries opened a riveting window into life in war-torn London. Private correspondence often reveals insights and historical context that we might otherwise not have known about events, perspectives, and intentions.

In John 17, we are given access to some of Jesus's private correspondence. This passage is a prayer that he prayed to his Father on the night before he died. In the first part of the prayer, Jesus prays for himself (see vv. 1–5). He then prays for his disciples (see vv. 6–19), after which he prays for the universal church—all those who will believe in Christ through the message of the gospel that would be shared by the disciples. What he prays for in this last portion is staggering:

> My prayer is not for them alone. I pray also for those who will believe in me through their message, that all of them may be *one*, Father, just as you are *in* me and I am *in* you. May they also be *in* us so that the world may believe that you have sent me. I have given them the glory that you gave me, that they may be *one* as we are *one*—I *in* them and you *in* me—so that they may be brought to complete unity. Then the world will know that you sent me and have loved them even as you have loved me. (John 17:20–23)

---

13. See John J. Hughes, "Perspectives on the Kingdom of God in Romans 14:17," in *Redeeming the Life of the Mind: Essays in Honor of Vern Poythress*, ed. John M. Frame, Wayne Grudem, and John J. Hughes (Wheaton, IL: Crossway, 2017), 358–84.

This is one of the most important passages in the entire Bible for understanding the nature and purpose of the church.

Notice, first of all, the pervasive concept of oneness. The words "one" or "in" (italicized) are used no fewer than eight times, and they always refer to the concept of unity. Jesus insists that the oneness of the church is grounded in the oneness of God. As we saw in part 1, God is Trinity: he is "one" God who has eternally existed as three distinct but inseparable persons. In the same way, the church is "one" church that exists as many distinct but inseparable persons. The unity of the church reflects the unity of God himself.

Second, this unity reflects the gospel. Notice what verse 23 is saying: "I *in* them and you *in* me—so that they may be brought to complete unity." As we saw in part 2, this is the heart of the gospel. Sin—humanity's attempt to remove the distinction between God and itself—led to a separation between God and humanity. In order to bridge the gap, God the Son assumed a distinct but inseparable human nature. Through his life, death, and resurrection, Jesus has united us to him through faith (him in us and us in him) and, in so doing, has united us to the triune God. This is glorious. The unity of the church flows from our union with Christ, which is the heart and the foundation of the gospel. This means that the unity of the church reflects the gospel.

When we grasp this, we can see why Jesus insists that church unity is essential to the credibility of our evangelism. Jesus's desire in verse 21 is "that the world may believe that you have sent me," and his purpose is verse 23 is that "the world will know that you sent me and have loved them even as you have loved me." This tells us that the unity of the church is one of the ways God reveals to unbelievers who he is and how he has made salvation possible. It is his global gospel billboard.

This is exactly what the apostle Paul teaches in his letter to the church in Ephesus. In Ephesians 2:11–3:6, Paul argues that the cross has reconciled not only humanity to God but also humans to one another. A fundamental division ran through ancient Near Eastern society between Jews and Gentiles. They called each other horrible names that would make us wince today. They hated each other and would not mingle or even eat together. And yet consider how Paul describes Jesus and his work: "For he himself is our peace, who has made the two groups one and has destroyed the barrier, the dividing wall of hostility" (Eph. 2:14). That is what Jesus has done, but notice how he has done it:

> His purpose was to create in himself one new humanity out of the two, thus making peace, and in one body to reconcile both of them to God through the cross, by which he put to death their hostility. (Eph. 2:15–16)

Jesus united Jews and Gentiles in himself. This is so important for understanding the source of true unity in diversity. Jesus has reconciled us to God *in himself* and *through his work* on the cross. He has done that both for those who were near (Jews) and for those who were far away (Gentiles), but the benefits of his work can only be accessed through union with Christ (see Eph. 2:17).

As we saw in part 4, all that Christ has done remains of no benefit to us as long as we are outside him. We must be united to Christ by faith. If we are not, we will not benefit from anything he has done. Yet, if we are united to him, we are also united to all other Christians, regardless of their religious, ethnic, or social background. I am a White British man who loves soccer (we call it football!) and hates oysters. But I have more in common with a Black Malawian Christian girl who hates soccer and loves shellfish than with a White British unbelieving man who shares all my tastes and interests. Indeed, I am united to that girl in a manner that trumps and transcends any other affinity I have along ethnic, social, or cultural lines because our union is founded in Christ. The same spiritual union that unites us to Christ also unites us to every other believer—distinctly but inseparably.

To look at it from another perspective, if we desire to separate ourselves from another Christian or another group of Christians, the only way we can do so is by separating ourselves from Christ. And if we do that, we are separating ourselves from his saving work and the reconciliation with God that he has achieved. Bridging the gap between ourselves and God is only possible if we are distinctly yet inseparably united to Christ and, in him, to every other believer.

The apostle Paul grasped the ground-breaking evangelistic significance of all this. In Ephesians 3, he digresses from the flow of his argument to discuss a "mystery." Now, in scriptural language, a mystery is not like a

Scooby-Doo story—a tough problem that the Mystery Inc. gang needs to solve. Rather, a biblical mystery is something that was once hidden but has now been revealed. According to Paul, the mystery that has been revealed in Christ is that "through the gospel the Gentiles are heirs together with Israel, members together of one body, and sharers together in the promise in Christ Jesus" (v. 6). This mystery has been revealed in the church—the multiethnic, multilingual, multicultural people of God—which means that the church, despite all her messiness and difficulty, is a visible display of God's glory to a watching world (see v. 10).

An illustration may help here. The church is like a diamond. When experts cut diamonds, they do so in such a way as to produce multiple facets. These facets are flat surfaces that are arranged in a geometrical pattern. This enables them to act like prisms, refracting the light and causing the gemstone to sparkle.

That is what the church is like. It is made up of multiple facets that are distinct in ethnicity and background. Each facet refracts the light of the gospel in a different way and interacts with the others, causing the gospel to sparkle through their lives lived together. We need one another, in all our glorious ethnic and cultural diversity, in order to show the sparkle of the gospel.

Separation from other Christians means separation from Christ

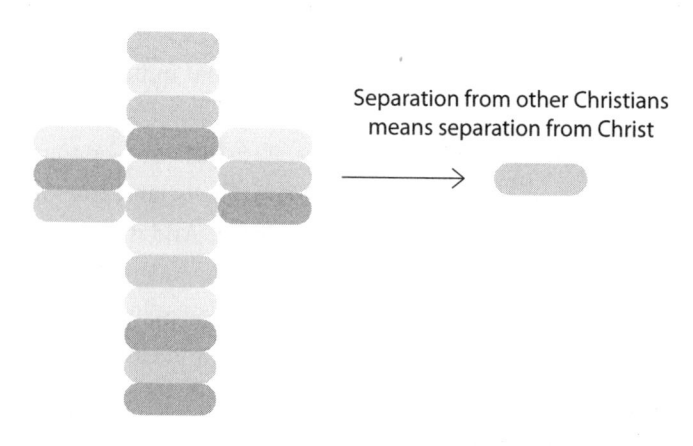

Fig. 17.1. One Lord and Savior of All

Living It Out: Glorious Diversity

Donald McGavran was wrong. Actually, let me qualify that. From a marketing perspective, he was probably right. We *are* attracted to people who are like us. Thus, a student church is more likely to attract students. A Chinese church is more likely to attract Chinese people, and a White American church is more likely to attract White Americans.

But there is a problem. What you win people with is what you win people to. If people are won to a church because of its whiteness, they will be won to whiteness, not Christ. If people are won to a church because of its Korean music, they will be won to Korean music, not Christ.

Moreover, intentionally monocultural churches obscure and even deny the truth of the gospel. Why? Because the very person who reconciles us to God—Jesus Christ—also reconciles us to people of every ethnicity and background. Irwyn Ince Jr. puts it so well: "The church is the living sign of the union of all things in Christ because he supernaturally reconciles us to God and to one another by the power of his Spirit. Refusing to pursue this reconciliation is akin to resisting the heart of God."[14] To deny the reconciling power of the gospel horizontally (between people) is to deny the reconciling power of the gospel vertically (between humanity and God). It is that serious.

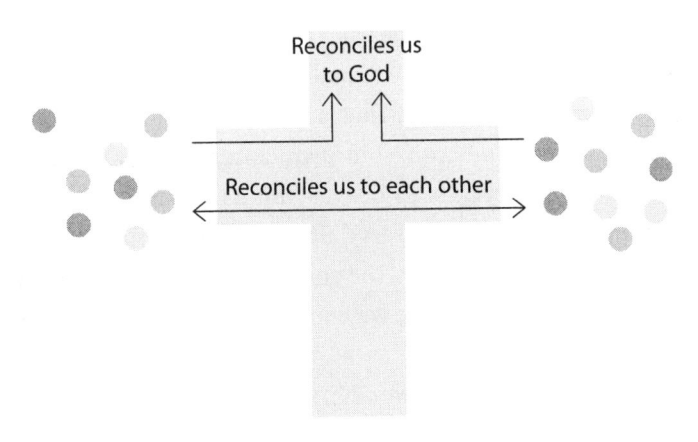

Fig. 17.2. Horizontal and Vertical Reconciliation through the Cross

14. Ince Jr., *The Beautiful Community*, 10.

This does not, however, mean that every ethnicity and background must be represented in every local church. That would be impossible. Rather, a local church should, as far as possible, reflect the demographic of its local community. For many churches, this community will include local residents. For others, especially those in urban centers, it may also include people who work or socialize close to where the church meets. Either way, to the degree that a local church does not reflect the diversity of its local community, it should seek to do the hard work of finding out why. Has it erected barriers that dissuade people of different ethnicities from accessing the church?

This work will not be easy. In fact, it may be very painful. But the gospel demands that we do it, and it graciously provides the tools that we need. What do I mean? Well, we ought to start by examining our own hearts, to look for the ethnic and cultural prejudice that lies within them.

Notice that I did not say to look for the prejudice that *may* lie within our hearts. The fall has corrupted every aspect of who we are, how we think, and how we act. This means that everyone harbors prejudice. Prejudice is an inevitable consequence of the fall. The problem is that our culture encourages us to hide and deny it. Our culture treats racial prejudice as an unforgivable sin—therefore, people feel pressure to deny the existence of prejudice rather than tackle it in their own hearts. The gospel frees us to name our prejudice, receive complete and free forgiveness for it, and then experience the healing power of Christ in our warped hearts.

The gospel also stirs the desire to make our churches more accessible. We like things that are familiar to us. That is natural, but our sinful hearts sometimes use this instinct to baptize our own cultural preferences as spiritual requirements.[15] This can be seen in everything from our style of corporate worship to the refreshments we serve after the service and the dress code of our greeters standing at the door. The gospel enables us to forgo our cultural preferences in order to prioritize welcoming people from different ethnicities, cultures, and backgrounds.

Celebrating diversity in our worship style, hospitality, and dress is important. This should not be forced. Hosting an annual "International Service" with Swahili songs is not the answer. Rather, consider the following:

---

15. See Ince Jr., 97–98.

- If 10 percent of our regulars are of East African heritage and wear culturally African clothes throughout the week, we need to ask why they don't wear those clothes at church on Sunday.
- If a third of our church is Hispanic, but our choir is all White, we need to ask why. Are there barriers that have hindered Hispanics from joining the choir? If so, can these be addressed, or should the choir be disbanded?
- If a quarter of our church is East Asian, but church lunches always consist of Southern BBQ, we need to make a change.
- We must not just accept the fact that our session is all White if a third of our church membership is non-White. There may be good reasons why the session is monoethnic, but we should not assume a good reason without investigating first.

In short, we need to do the hard work of "prob[ing] our preferences to find out whether they help or hinder diverse people from experiencing welcome."[16]

We have seen that a multiethnic church confirms and commends the gospel. It has evangelistic power, and it fuels cross-cultural mission. This is clear from the history of the church in Antioch. Acts 11 shows us that Antioch was the first church to gather cross-culturally and that this diversity was represented in its leadership (see Acts 13:1).[17] Having gathered cross-culturally, it also became the first church to send cross-culturally, sending Saul and Barnabas on their first missionary journey to Cyprus, Lycia, and Galatia. Surely this is no coincidence. When we embrace the truth that the good news of Jesus is for people of every ethnicity, we live out the Great Commission: sending people to make disciples of all ethnic groups (see Matt. 28:19).

Some suggest, however, that cross-cultural mission is divisive. The claim that the gospel is for people of all ethnicities, cultures, and backgrounds undermines the unity of humankind. Lesslie Newbigin was a British missionary to India in the twentieth century and frequently faced such accusations. He responded, "Christians also want the unity of humankind, but it is not to be found by just repeating abstract words like justice, love, peace. We Christians

---

16. See Ince Jr., 126.
17. As Ince notes, "Structural inclusion of people of color into influential positions is an aspect of the proper exercise of power and hospitality." Ince Jr., 138.

believe the unity of the human race will be found in the Man Jesus Christ, in whom God was reconciling the whole world."[18] That is the burden of this chapter.

We crave a unity that does not erode the beauty and value of our distinctiveness. Our society's attempts to find that unity through such abstract concepts as "love" and "common humanity" ultimately fail. True unity is found in only one place—Jesus. He brings people together across cultural and ethnic divides, that they may be reconciled to himself as "one new humanity" (Eph. 2:15). Jesus makes the many one in himself, and he enables them to live out their unity by transforming their attitudes toward one another. The good news of Jesus is for everyone. It preserves our individuality while radically uniting us and allowing us to reflect our unity as we bear the fruit of the Spirit (see Gal. 5:22–23).

In February 2015, twenty-one men were led onto a beach in Sirte, Libya, and forced to stand in a line close to where the sea was lapping the shore.[19] They were dressed in orange jumpsuits, and twenty-one men dressed in black accompanied them. The captives were Egyptian Coptic Christians who had been kidnapped by the Islamic State in Libya. But one of them stood out—unlike the others, he was Black. His captors questioned him. His name was Matthew, and he was from Ghana. He was not a Copt, so they said he could go. But Matthew replied, "No, I am like them. I am a Christian." And with that, he knelt on the beach and was beheaded alongside his twenty Christian brothers.

By the world's standards, Matthew had nothing in common with the other men. But he was united with them in Christ, which means that he was one with them in life, death, and future glory.

Making It Personal

1. What examples of ethnic prejudice have you experienced or witnessed in your workplace, school, or neighborhood? In your Christian community or church?

---

18. Quoted by Tim Keller in his sermon "A New Church for the City," preached at Redeemer Presbyterian Church on November 7, 2010.
19. I am grateful to Glynn Harrison for pointing me to this amazing example of oneness in Christ.

2. What are some of the ways you've seen ethnic prejudice addressed helpfully or unhelpfully in your church or Christian community?
3. Where do you see your own prejudice? How can the gospel help realign your heart to seek unity in Christ?
4. How could you help foster more ethnic unity in your church? How could you intentionally develop friendships across ethnic boundaries?
5. If you're in the ethnic majority at your church, how could you help create a welcoming environment for ethnic minorities?
6. If you're studying this book in a small group, discuss which ethnic and cultural groups are currently represented in your group and consider what additional groups are conspicuously absent. Why might this be the case?

Further Reading for Part 6

Beynon, Graham, and Jane Tooher. *Embracing Complementarianism: Turning Biblical Convictions into Positive Church Culture.* London: The Good Book Company, 2022.

Clowney, Edmund P. *The Church.* Contours of Christian Theology. Leicester, UK: IVP, 1995.

Ince, Irwyn L., Jr. *The Beautiful Community: Unity, Diversity, and the Church at Its Best.* Downers Grove, IL: IVP, 2020.

Linne, Shai. *The New Reformation: Finding Hope in the Fight for Ethnic Unity.* Chicago: Moody Publishers, 2021.

CONCLUSION

John Lennon urged us to "imagine" a world in which there was no more war, a place where everybody lived as "one." That song struck a chord with many people because it expressed a universal longing for unity across gender, age, ethnic, and cultural lines. But that unity in diversity has always seemed to be tantalizingly out of reach. When governments seek to cultivate it, they invariably fail. Even in our families, we struggle to accommodate meaningful diversity, and our society seems to be more divided and demoralized than ever.

In part 1 of the book, we explored the reason for our widespread longing for unity in diversity. We were created by a God who is himself unity in diversity. The God of the Bible is one God who has eternally existed in three distinct but inseparable persons—at the heart of the universe is a personal being who is relational within himself. God's triune nature explains our longing for relationship and our attraction to the idea of unity in diversity. It also reminds us that dignity and worth are found in who we are, not in what we do.

In part 2, we saw why unity in diversity appears to be so elusive. We, the worshipers, were created to be distinct from God, the worshiped One. Had we fulfilled that purpose, humanity would have remained inseparable from God. Tragically, however, the first man and woman rebelled against God. They desired to "be like God" (Gen. 3:5)—a rejection of distinction—and this rebellion resulted in a radical separation from God and each other. This is the root and the cause of all the relational friction we experience in the world, and it explains why unity in diversity appears so difficult to attain.

The good news of the gospel is that God the Son has united himself to a human nature that is distinct but inseparable from his divine nature.

The separation caused by the fall has been wonderfully undone in Christ's person and by his perfect obedience and substitutionary death. Through the resurrection of Christ, we have been restored to the inseparable yet distinct relationship with God for which we were created.

In part 3, we explored how the idea of "distinction without separation" enables us to navigate the complex relationship between God's sovereignty and human responsibility. In every situation, God is sovereign and human beings are responsible for what we voluntarily do, but God stands behind good and evil in distinct and asymmetrical ways. This allows us to explain why there are absolute moral standards that transcend cultural contexts. It also helps us approach discernment, prayer, and evangelism, and it offers a framework for walking through suffering with both realism and hope.

In part 4, we looked at how "distinction without separation" shapes our identity as Christians. The good news of the gospel is that we receive Christ and, in him, justification, sanctification, and adoption. The church has struggled to understand these three aspects of our union with Christ—either mixing them together or separating them from one another.

It is important that justification, sanctification, and adoption remain distinct because sanctification is transformative, while justification and adoption are declarative. But they must also not be separated. All three are inseparable aspects of our union with Christ. Justification and adoption give us an external identity that is rooted in Christ and his finished work, making them secure and immutable. Sanctification is an inward and emerging experience of who we truly are. A right understanding of our union with Christ provides a compelling answer to our culture's desire for an identity that is concrete, externally affirmed, and inwardly experienced. That is exactly what we receive in the gospel by virtue of our union with Christ.

The distinct but inseparable formula helps us understand how we grow as Christians, as we saw in part 5. The Holy Spirit is the effective cause of Christian growth. He indwells all believers and conforms us to the likeness of Christ. He fulfills that work through the instrumental means of grace: the ministry of the Word, the ministry of the sacraments, and prayer.

The Holy Spirit accompanies the means of grace and is inseparable from them, but he works in them to achieve distinct ends: blessing those who come with faith and judging those who don't. This means that we should approach the means of grace with prayer (because we depend on God's grace) and with expectation because the Spirit has promised to accompany them with power in order to bless us.

In the final part of the book, we considered how the distinct but inseparable formula guides us through some of the most difficult issues in the church today. In the Reformed church, there has been such an emphasis on Word-ministry gifts (especially preaching) that we have neglected other gifts. We need to recognize that we are one body with many parts: distinct in function but inseparable in purpose as we seek to glorify God and enjoy him forever. This requires us to identify and cultivate gifts in others and to facilitate the use of those gifts in church life. The past decade has seen rapid changes in the way that people communicate and relate with one another. We need to harness the distinct gifts that we find in the church today to meet contemporary challenges.

We also saw how the distinct but inseparable formula helps us to achieve unity within the church in some of the most divisive areas. Our society is currently divided between those who want to separate the genders (classical feminism) and those who seek to mix them (the transgender movement). What at first seems like an incredibly controversial position—biblical complementarianism—is in fact a radically appealing alternative to the current polarities. The church needs to regain its confidence in complementarianism and unashamedly celebrate God's design for men and women.

Finally, we saw how God's purposes for the church satisfy our society's deep longing for unity in diversity. In Christ, God has saved people from every nation, tribe, and tongue. He doesn't require his people to conform to particular cultural norms or customs but, rather, has purposed that we should worship him as one body while retaining our distinctive ethnic, cultural, and linguistic identities. That is the consummation pictured in the book of Revelation—the certain future toward which the church is heading. Wonderfully, we get the chance to experience this unity now—in the local church—as we display God's glory through our distinct but inseparable communities.

This most wonderful truth is also the most challenging aspect of the book. Our society longs for perfect unity. Our musicians sing about it; our politicians promise it; our artists draw it; but only the church can achieve it. We will achieve perfect unity on that glorious day when Christ returns and transforms us into his likeness. Until that day, we are called to pursue unity as we hold out the good news of Jesus.

Our God is unity in diversity. He desires to unite his diverse creation as one in Christ. We get to participate in that now as his distinct but inseparable people—those who pursue perfect unity in the church. Will you rise to meet the challenge?

GLOSSARY

adoption. The declarative act by which we are made members of God's family.

Apollinarianism. The view, associated with Apollinarius, that God the Son assumed a human body but not a higher soul and a rational mind because God the Son had taken their place.

apprehension. To know true things about something without knowing it exhaustively.

Arianism. The view, associated with Arius, that the Son was a created being and not of the same being as the Father.

communion. The lived experience of union with Christ that is mutual. It involves giving and receiving, loving and being loved.

complementarianism. The teaching that men and women are equal in dignity and worth but distinct in function in marriage and the church.

comprehension. To know something exhaustively.

consubstantiation. The Lutheran teaching that the physical body and blood of Jesus are present in, with, and under the bread and the wine in the Lord's Supper.

determinism. The view that everything in the universe is determined by external forces.

Docetism. The view that the Word only appeared to be human but was not truly human.

ex opere operato. The Roman Catholic teaching that the means of grace convey grace even if the person receiving the means does not come with faith. The Latin phrase literally means "from the work worked."

human responsibility. Human beings are morally responsible and will be held accountable for their thoughts, words, and actions.

incarnation, the. The act of God the Son uniting to himself a fully human nature. Derived from the Latin *in carne*, meaning "in flesh."

indeterminism. The view that human beings are autonomous and that external powers (natural or supernatural) do not have any bearing on our actions.

inseparable operation. The teaching that, in every action of God, the three persons of the Trinity work inseparably together.

justification. The forensic (legal) declaration of right standing with God.

modalism. The view that God has existed in three different modes of being during three different periods: the Father in the Old Testament, the Son in the New Testament, and the Spirit in the church age.

Nestorianism. The view, associated with Nestorius, that the incarnation involved a "conjunction" of the two natures of Christ rather than a true union of the natures.

ontology. The nature of being and existence.

person. The term used to emphasize the distinction between Father, Son, and Holy Spirit. In modern usage, it implies separate individuals, but in Trinitarian theology, it conveys a personal yet inseparable understanding of the Trinity.

redemption. The language, originating in the slave market, used to describe the act by which humans are purchased from slavery to sin and Satan through the payment of a price.

sanctification. The transformative act of being made holy. It has past (declarative), present (progressive), and future (perfective) orientations.

silver bullet. Something that instantly solves a longstanding problem. Derived from the folkloric trope that only a silver bullet could slay a werewolf or a witch.

sovereignty. Supreme power and authority that is in control.

transubstantiation. The Roman Catholic teaching that, in the Lord's Supper, the bread and the wine become the physical body and blood of Jesus Christ.

tritheism. The view that God is three separate beings—three gods.

union with Christ. The real, spiritual union of believers to Christ by the power of the Holy Spirit.

Don't Miss the Blessings of the Faith Series

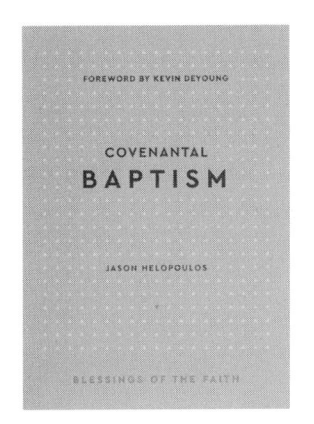

COVENANTAL BAPTISM
JASON HELOPOULOS

"A truly remarkable, page-turning book that . . . persuasively and winsomely presents a robust defense of the baptism of infants of believers."
—**Joel R. Beeke**, President, Puritan Reformed Theological Seminary

"In his clear and witty style, Rhodes not only informs in this book—he also inspires."
—**D. Blair Smith**, Associate Professor of Systematic Theology, Reformed Theological Seminary

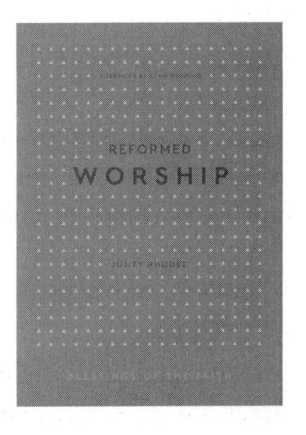

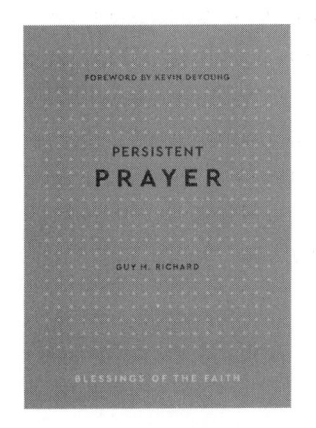

REFORMED WORSHIP

PERSISTENT PRAYER
GUY H. RICHARD

"I love this book! . . . Thank you, Guy, for giving us such clear answers, anchored in the Scriptures, for why we should pray. What a gift."
—**Crawford W. Loritts Jr.**, Author; Speaker; Radio Host

Also from P&R Publishing

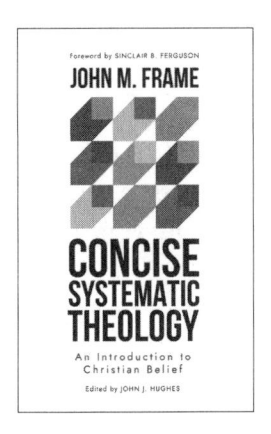

This concise, practical, and devotional introduction to Reformed systematics now features study questions, memory verses, and additional resources to help readers to develop a thoroughly biblical framework for understanding and applying Christian doctrine. Revised and enhanced edition of John Frame's *Salvation Belongs to the Lord*.

"John Frame is the most creative conservative evangelical theologian of his generation, and I am delighted to recommend to another generation this excellent summary of what Christians believe. Here is the perfect combination of biblical fidelity, pedagogical utility, prose clarity, doctrinal profundity, and spiritual fecundity. Five out of five stars!"
—**Kevin J. Vanhoozer**, Research Professor of Systematic Theology, Trinity Evangelical Divinity School

"This is . . . a very practical and devotional book. . . . Read [it] to grow in wisdom; read it to cut through all the cultural noise about Christianity and get right to the heart of the Bible's message; and perhaps most importantly of all, read it to cultivate a deeper love for our extraordinary God."
—**Christopher Watkin**, Senior Lecturer in French Studies, Monash University

Did you find this book helpful?
Consider writing a review online.
We appreciate your feedback!

Or write to P&R at editorial@prpbooks.com
with your comments. We'd love to hear from you.